WILL,
FREEDOM AND POWER

ANTHONY KENNY

WILL, FREEDOM AND POWER

BOOKS
10 East 53d St., New York 10022
(a division of Harper & Row Publishers, Inc.)

ISBN 0–06–493639–2

PRINTED IN GREAT BRITAIN

CONTENTS

PREFACE   vi

I.   The Mind and the Will   1

II.   The Will in Philosophical Tradition   12

III.   The Imperative Theory of the Will   29

IV.   Voluntariness and Intentionality   46

V.   Practical Reasoning and Rational Appetite   70

VI.   Between Reason and Action   97

VII.   Spontaneity, Indifference, and Ability   122

VIII.   Freedom and Determinism   145

BIBLIOGRAPHY   162

INDEX   165

PREFACE

Twelve years ago I published a book with the title *Action, Emotion and Will*. In that book I presented a theory of action and volition while deliberately abstaining from any consideration of the traditional problem of the freedom of the will. In the present work I propose to extend and modify that theory in the light of criticism and discussion during the intervening years, and to apply my conclusions to elucidating the nature of freedom and its relation to determinism. The central theme of the book will be that the human will is the ability to act for reasons, and that its freedom derives from the special characteristics of practical reasoning.

The majority of the present work consists of material which is here published for the first time. Parts of chapters I, III, V and VIII are developments of published papers: 'The Origin of the Soul' (in Longuet-Higgins *et al.*, *The Development of Mind*, Edinburgh, 1974); 'Intention and Purpose' (*Journal of Philosophy*, 1966); 'Practical Inference' (*Analysis* supplement, 1966); 'Freedom, Spontaneity and Indifference' (in *Essays on Freedom of Action*, ed. Honderich, London, 1973) respectively. I am grateful for permission to reprint portions of those papers.

Chapters of the book were read as papers to philosophical societies and seminars in Oxford, Cornell, Princeton, Calvin College, Helsinki and elsewhere. I am grateful to those who took part in the discussions on those occasions. I also wish to thank friends who commented on draft sections, especially Professor G. E. M. Anscombe, Professor P. T. Geach, Mrs. P. R. Foot, Dr. Peter Hacker, Dr. Anselm Müller and Dr. Joseph Raz, and also my wife who read through the whole manuscript in draft and corrected many errors and infelicities.

31 January 1975

I

THE MIND AND THE WILL

'The long disputed question concerning liberty and necessity' is, if we are to believe David Hume, 'the most contentious question of metaphysics, the most contentious science'. According to Samuel Johnson 'All theory is against the freedom of the will, all experience for it.' The centuries since Hume and Johnson have seen no diminution of the conflict between experience and theory or of the contention between metaphysicians. The progress of science has led many to question whether mankind can continue to claim the unique autonomy it has always prized. Is there room for genuine freedom in a universe governed by scientific law? May not our experiences of choice, of effort and of guilt be illusions born of ignorance, dreams which will be dispelled when in the next generation or two the social sciences draw level with their physical counterparts? Can a continued belief in the freedom of the will be more than an empty and blinkered challenge to the inevitable progress of science?

We cannot answer these question without knowing what we mean when we speak of the freedom of the will. What is this thing, the will, that is being claimed to be free? The traditional answer was that the will was a faculty of the mind. Apart from an unexpected revival by the school of Chomsky the psychology of faculties has long been out of fashion. Certainly, if a faculty is thought of as a ghostly operative force in the mysterious medium of the mind, or as a homunculus pulling levers in the signal box of the brain, then faculties are figments of the imagination that will not survive serious reflection. And it has been a truism since the time of Molière that one does not give a scientific explanation of a phenomenon by assigning it to an appropriate power. None the less there is, I believe, a profound truth in the ancient theory that the will is a faculty of the mind. But this in turn can only be assessed if we attach a precise significance to the word 'mind'.

The mind is the capacity to acquire intellectual abilities. Two things must be noticed about this definition. First mind is a capacity, not an activity. Thus it is possible to say that babies have minds even though they do not yet display intellectual activities of the appropriate kind. Secondly, mind is not only a capacity, but a capacity for capacities. Knowledge of a language such as English is itself a capacity or ability: an ability whose exercise is the speaking, understanding, reading of English. To have a mind is to have a capacity at a further remove from actualization: to have the capacity to acquire such abilities as a knowledge of English.

By intellectual activities I mean activities involving the creation and utilization of symbols. On this definition, clearly the use of language, the solution of a mathematical problem, the painting of a portrait are, as we would expect, intellectual activities. The definition leaves many things uncertain at the borderline, but this is all to the good, for so does the ordinary concept of mind that we are trying to capture in a definition. On the other hand all the things which are well within the realm of what we regard as mental activities—like physics, philosophy, and poetry—are well within the bounds laid down by this definition.

Two questions which have exercised philosophers are whether animals, or some animals, have minds, and whether computers have minds.

In Nevada and California and elsewhere large claims are made for the linguistic achievements of chimpanzees, claims which are the subject of keen debate among psychologists and linguists. If anyone is left in doubt by our definition whether gifted chimpanzees like Washoe and Sarah have minds, it is because he is in doubt whether they are using language, and thus manifesting an ability for intellectual activity; he is in doubt therefore whether they possess the capacity for acquiring such abilities which is what is traditionally meant by 'mind'.

According to this definition, computers very definitely do not have minds. They do, in a sense, operate with symbols, but *our* symbols; they are not symbols for them, it is we and not computers who confer the meaning on the symbols. That is why the definition included a reference to the *creation* of symbols. To have a mind is to have the capacity to acquire the ability to operate with symbols in such a way that it is one's own activity that makes them symbols and confers meaning on them.

Not only does the definition have a broad borderline, it is in a way infinitely open. For many different things may be described as operating with symbols, and we cannot set any bounds to the possibility of the invention of new types of symbolic operation. At no time can we draw a boundary around the forms of symbolic activity current at that time and say: 'Those activities, and no others, count as intelligent activity.' Nor can we be sure that we shall ever be able to isolate from them some common element and say: 'Anything which is intelligence must have this element', unless we leave the notion of 'element' as open as the notions of 'symbol', 'meaning' and 'activity' as I am using them.

Given this account of the nature of the mind, what is the place of the will? Traditionally the intellect and the will stood side by side as the two great faculties of the mind. Traditionally, too, the will is thought of as the locus of autonomy: of the human agent's possession of personal, long-term ideals. These features of the traditional picture fit well with our definition. The pursuit of self-selected goals that go beyond the immediate environment in space and time is not possible without the use of symbols for the distant, the remote, and the universal. And on the other hand, the use of symbols itself involves purposes which go beyond the temporal and spatial present. First of all, meaning something is a matter of intending, and intending involves having purposes: again, meaning is done in accordance with rules, and rules are of their nature capable of repeated application in diverse circumstances. Secondly, to use something as a symbol and not as a tool is to use it in such a way that any effect which it may have on the environment lacks the immediacy and regularity characteristic of physical causality. So the mind, as I have defined it, is a volitional as well as a cognitive capacity: it includes the will as well as the intellect.

However, there is an important qualification to be made here. If we say that the will is a faculty it seems that what we are saying is that a being has a will if it has the power to intend, choose, decide, enjoy, regret and so on. (On this account it will be clear that human beings have wills and clear that leaves have not; about crabs and cuckoos, not to mention the higher animals, the question is once again, for the moment, left open.) But reflection makes clear that it is not quite right to regard the will as a faculty. At least the will is not a set of capacities in the way in which the intellect is a set of capacities. To possess intelligence is to possess, *inter alia*, the capacity to learn how to do sums; but there is no performance which stands to the faculty of the will in the relationship which the performance of doing sums stands to the faculty of the intellect. For intending, choosing, deciding, enjoying, regretting are not activities in the way that doing arithmetic, and even learning to do arithmetic, are activities. One intends, chooses, decides *to do* something, enjoys *doing* it, regrets *having done* it. The verbs we used in attempting to characterize the set of capacities which made up the will were all verbs which needed completion by another verb. 'He is doing arithmetic' may be a complete characterization of a man's action at a particular time in a way in which 'He is intending, he is choosing, he is deciding, he is enjoying, he is regretting' are not.

We can test and measure the intelligence of different human beings, up to a point, by observing their proficiency in suitably selected tasks. Such testing, no doubt, involves a degree of tightening up, and possibly tendentious redefinition, of the everyday concept of 'intelligence'; but the concept produced by this exercise is a perfectly comprehensible one and is useful for many of the same purposes as the everyday concept is. But it seems that no amount of rigorization of the concept of 'will' would put us in a position to allot candidates volitional quotients as we can allot them IQs. We can, of course, test and measure such things as the perseverance of candidates in particular tasks. But in testing such things we are not testing candidates' wills in the way in which we are testing their intelligence in getting them to spot the odd man out in a series. For the abandonment of an attempt to solve a problem is just as much a voluntary action as the continuance of the attempt; where as the failure to spot the odd man out is not just as much an intelligent performance as the successful spotting.

If we are to regard the will as a faculty, it seems that we must regard the abilities of which it consists as in a sense second-order abilities; as abilities to do things in a certain way, namely voluntarily or intentionally. The consideration of the will as a faculty thus leads to the notion of voluntary and intentional action, which will be our concern in a later chapter.

There are two ways in which my definition of mind, traditional though it is, departs from familiar approaches to the definition of mentality. First, I do not take the making and using of tools as by itself an exhibition of mentality. Assisting oneself by inert instruments in the performance of an activity may or may not be a manifestation of mind; that depends, among other things, on whether the activity itself is. Thus the use of clocks to tell the time or the use of a pen to write a letter is an intellectual activity; the use of a stick to shake a banana from a tree is not.

Secondly, in my definition of mind I have not said anything about consciousness. There are at least two sharply distinct things which may be meant by that term. The first is the consciousness which is the exercise of our capacities for perception: the awareness of, and ability to respond to, changes in the environment which is given us by the senses like hearing, seeing, smelling and tasting. The second is self-consciousness: the knowledge of what one is doing and why. In human beings self-consciousness presupposes sense-consciousness but is not identical with it. Self-consciousness presupposes also, I should maintain, the possession of language; one cannot know how to talk about oneself without knowing how to talk, and one cannot think about oneself without being able to talk about oneself.

This last can be shown without appealing to any general thesis about the relationship between talking and thinking. There is a particular reason connecting talk about oneself and thought about oneself. A dog may well think that his master is at the door: but unless a dog masters a language it is hard to see how he can think *that he is thinking that* his master is at the door. There is nothing that the dog could do that could express the difference beween the two thoughts: 'My master is at the door', and 'I am thinking that my master is at the door'. If I am right that self-consciousness is thus intimately connected with language, then I can take account of the tradition that regards self-consciousness as closely linked with mentality without mentioning it specially in my definition. On the other hand, by distinguishing between mentality and sense-consciousness I am able to do justice both to my admiration for Descartes and my affection for my dog. I can agree with the former that animals do not have minds while according to the latter a full measure of non-mechanical consciousness.

The definition of the mind as a capacity is likely to be rejected as too austere and abstract, as ignoring the most obvious and fundamental fact about the mind. Surely the mind is not just a faculty: it is an immaterial and private world, the locus of our secret thoughts, the auditorium of our interior monologues, the theatre in which our dreams are staged and our plans rehearsed. Defining the mind as a capacity ignores all this: it is a dogmatic behaviouristic failure to look the obvious in the eye.

It would be folly to deny that human beings can keep their thoughts secret, can talk to themselves without making any noise, can sketch figures before their mind's eye instead of on pieces of paper. The appropriate name for the capacity for mental imagery of this kind—visual, audio, motor and other imagery—is the *imagination*. The imagination, no less than the mind, is a capacity or faculty. Particular exercises of imagination are psychological events, occurring at particular times and places; they are experiences, in relation to which the subject is in a uniquely authoritative position. (The authority he has, though, is the authority of the judge, not of the witness.) These psychological events occur with great frequency in our lives; they may play a greater or lesser part in our lives according to the active or contemplative nature of our temperament and vocation.

There is a perfectly natural use of the word 'mental' in which exercises of the imagination may be called 'mental events'. When children are asked to work out arithmetical problems in imagination rather than on paper they are said to be doing 'mental arithmetic'. This sense of 'mental', though natural, is misleading. What proves that children have minds is that they can learn to do arithmetic at all; being able to do the working in interior monologue is a comparatively unimportant extra. Doing a difficult sum on paper may be a greater proof of intellect than doing an easy one in the head. It is the nature of the skill exercised that is the crucial matter; the ability to exercise it silently and motionlessly is an added grace, no more. And so with interior monologue in general. The acquisition of the ability to talk *about* oneself, as I have said, is enormously significant; the acquisition of the ability to talk *to* oneself is by comparison merely a matter of convenience. A society which differed from ours only in that everyone thought aloud all the time instead of thinking silently would be perfectly conceivable, equally intellectual, merely unbearably noisy.

No doubt, performance at mental arithmetic is a better guide to arithmetical talent, for any given problem, than the writing of sums in a book. But that is not because of anything specially significant about talking to oneself. Asked what 17×12 is, one child may have to work out on paper, one may have to recite tables in his head, the third may answer '204' in a flash. Other things being equal, it is the third that is the best arithmetician; but it is the second in whom the arithmetic is mental in the sense in which deliberation, pain, and visual imagery are mental. The test of arithmetical skill is not 'mentality' in this sense, but the ability to get by without pencil and paper.

The mental events which are the exercises of the imagination occur, as remarked, at particular times and places: a child may do a sum in his head while he is sitting at his desk, just as he may see a kestrel while running in the playground. We speak of mental arithmetic as being done 'in the head', but this, of course, is not to give a further localization which is more precise than the localization 'at his desk'. The head is the locus of the imagination only in this sense: that the things we imagine ourselves doing are things which we do quite literally with our heads or parts of them. When we talk silently to ourselves we imagine ourselves talking; and talking is done with the tongue, lips and palate, so that the imagined talking is felt in those and connected areas. We imagine ourselves seeing, which we do with our eyes, and hearing, which we do with our ears. Not all exercises of the imagination are 'in the head' in this sense: just as a pain may be felt in the back, or an itch between the toes, similarly when we imagine such a pain, or such an itch, it is in the back, or between the toes, and not 'in the head' that we imagine it. Still less, of course, are all exercises of consciousness 'in the head': houses, trees, clouds, rainbows, mirages and after images are all in different ways seen 'out there', just as brass bands, whispers and echoes are all heard 'out there'. Of course we know that without the activity of the brain, neither the intellect, the imagination nor the senses would function; but that is irrelevant to the sense in which mental arithmetic is done 'in the head'. Someone who thought, as Aristotle did, that it was the heart which performed the physiological functions now correctly localized in the brain, would have just as good and bad reasons as we have for localization of the exercises of the imagination 'in the head'.

What is the relation of the imagination, as just described, and the mind, as I earlier defined it? Principally this: that one of the things we frequently imagine ourselves doing is uttering words; one of the most frequent exercises of the imagination is the fragmentary interior monologue so artfully described by James Joyce. The use of language in the imagination is, no more than but also no less than the use of language in public, a mark of the possession of a mind. Artistic and non-linguistic intellectual activity also can be planned, rehearsed, and monitored in the imagination, and this too is an exercise of capacities which are mental in the strict sense.

To while away a crossing of the Irish Sea, Lord Macaulay repeated to himself the first five books of *Paradise Lost*. This feat was an exercise of memory, of intellect, and of imagination. Clearly, it was a fantastic feat of memory: but had he found his way through a particularly complex maze after a single journey —as no doubt he would—this would have been equally a feat of memory without necessarily involving the other faculties. In so far as he understood and appreciated what he was reciting, he was exercising his intellect (and therefore his mind in the strict sense). In that the whole performance went on under his breath, out of consideration for his fellow passengers on the steam packet, it was an exercise of the imagination. Of course in that *Paradise Lost*, unlike the *Lays of Ancient Rome*, was not his own composition, what he did was not an exercise of the imagination in the grander sense in which that means the faculty for artistic creation. But that faculty, while more precious than the more lowly faculty we have been considering, is less widespread and therefore less likely to be confused with the mind which is the mark of a rational animal.

My account of mind is, as I say, a very traditional one. It traces its ancestry back at least to Plato. In the tradition dominated by Plato the mind is thought of as being above all the ability to know universal ideas and eternal truths. Many philosophers have thought the belief that beyond our symbols in mathematics and philosophy there are such sublime entities can only be due to a misunderstanding of the nature of symbolism. Perhaps so: but after all Frege, the greatest philosopher of logic in modern times, thought that Plato was basically right. This must surely make one hesitate to take sides definitely against Plato.

Whatever the truth be here, my definition leaves the question open. If the mind is the capacity to operate with symbols, and if the way we operate with symbols is correctly understood in the way that Plato and Frege understood it, then the Platonic account of the mind is to that extent correct.

In several places Plato argues, and in this he has had many followers throughout the centuries, that if the mind can know the eternal and changeless then the mind must itself be essentially eternal and changeless, and at the very least be an immortal entity that can survive the death of the body. To get this conclusion Plato needs not only the premiss that the mind is the capacity to know the eternal, but also the premiss that like can only be known by like. There seems to me to be some truth in this archaic dictum if suitably reinterpreted: for example, if something is to be said to have knowledge of the multiplication table, it need not necessarily have the structure of the multiplication table (it may not even be clear what this would mean), but it must be capable of an output which is isomorphic to the multiplication table. But the thesis that the knower must have the same properties as the known is plausible only so far as it applies to the structural properties of the knowledge and its object; it concerns the content of knowledge and not the mode of knowing. The Platonists have never provided any good reason for thinking that there cannot be fugitive acquaintance with unchanging objects and temporary grasps of eternal truths. There seems no more reason to deny mortal knowledge of immortal verity than to deny the possibility of a picture in fireworks of the Rock of Gibraltar.

If the Platonist argument for the immortality of the mind embodies a fallacious inference, its conclusion seems to embody a conceptual confusion. If the mind is a capacity, we must ask not only what it is a capacity for but also what it is a capacity of; and the answer seems to be that it is a capacity of a certain kind of body. If this is so, then the notion of a disembodied mind is the notion of a capacity which is not anything's capacity. This seems to be as nonsensical as the notion of the Cheshire cat's smile without the Cheshire cat.

In a later chapter I shall discuss in some detail the nature of powers and capacities. But in this first chapter it is necessary to make some brief remarks to remove possible confusions about the claim that the mind is a capacity. There are two things which a capacity must be distinguished from: its exercise, and its vehicle. Consider the capacity of whisky to intoxicate. The possession of this capacity is clearly distinct from its exercise: the whisky possesses the capacity while it is standing harmlessly in the bottle, but it only begins to exercise it after being imbibed. The vehicle of this capacity to intoxicate is the alcohol that the whisky contains: it is the ingredient in virtue of which the whisky has the power to intoxicate. The vehicle of a power need not be a substantial ingredient like alcohol which can be physically separated from the possessor of the power, though it is in such cases that the distinction between a power and its vehicle is most obvious (one cannot, for example, weigh the power of whisky to intoxicate as one can weigh the alcohol it contains). Take the less exciting power which my wedding ring has of fitting on my finger. It has this power in virtue of having the size and shape it has, and size and shape are not modal, relational, potential properties in the same way as *being able to fit on my finger* is. They are not the power but the vehicle of the power. The connection between a power and its vehicle may be a necessary or a contingent one. It is a contingent matter, discovered by experiment, that alcohol is the vehicle of intoxication; but it is a conceptual truth that a round peg has the power to fit into a round hole.

Throughout the history of philosophy there has been a tendency for philosophers—especially scientifically-minded philosophers—to attempt to reduce potentialities to actualities. But there have been two different forms of reductionism, often combined and often confused, depending on whether the attempt was to reduce a power to its exercise or to its vehicle. Hume when he said that the distinction between a power and its exercise was wholly frivolous wanted to reduce powers to their exercises. Descartes when he attempted to identify all the powers of bodies with their geometrical properties wanted to reduce powers to their vehicles.

But if it is important to distinguish between powers and their exercises and vehicles it is important also not to err on the other side. A power or capacity must not be thought of as something in its own right, for instance as a flimsy actuality or insubstantial vehicle. The difference between power and its exercise or vehicle is a category difference, not a difference like that between solid and shadow. To hypostatize a power, to think of a power, say, as something which, while remaining numerically the same, might pass from one possessor to another is one way of erring on the anti-reductionist side, an error which has recently been aptly named 'transcendentalism'. In the Andersen fairy-tale the witch takes the old wife's gift of the gab and gives it to the water-butt. Less picturesque, but equally absurd, examples of transcendentalism can be found in the pages of many great philosophers.

The mind is a capacity, and the philosophical errors which occur in dealing with capacities in general occur in a particularly vivid way with regard to the mind. Behaviourism, when it takes the extreme form of identifying mind with behaviour, is a form of exercise-reductionism: treating the complex second-order capacity, which is the mind, as if it was identical with its particular exercises in behaviour. Materialism, when it takes the extreme form of identifying mind with brain, or with the central nervous system, is a form of vehicle-reductionism: reducing my mental capacities to the structural parts and features of my body in virtue of which I possess those capacities. The Platonist belief in immortality, on the other hand, is a form of transcendentalism: for only a transcendentalist can believe that a capacity can be separated from its possessor, or pass from one possessor to another by incarnation in successive different bodies.

The theory of the will which I will present in this book will be traditional without being Platonist. It will resemble the theory developed out of Aristotelian material by St. Thomas Aquinas and later medieval philosophers, rather more than it will resemble the view of classical post-renaissance philosophers. However, I shall try to free it from the Platonist elements which it incorporated in medieval times; and I shall try to incorporate into my presentation insights of contemporary philosophers. This will be the easier in that it was reflection on contemporary problems which brought me to see the very substantial degree of truth in the ancient theory.

I shall first present the theory in a historical form, setting it out in the next chapter and contrasting it with rival traditions; in succeeding chapters I shall develop the particular elements in contemporary terms and with the minimum of historical reference.

II

THE WILL IN PHILOSOPHICAL TRADITION

In modern philosophical tradition there have been two dominant conceptions of the will, one introvert and one extrovert. The introvert conception can be illustrated from Descartes, Hume, and William James. The extrovert tradition is represented, in different ways, by Wittgenstein, Austin, and Ryle.

Descartes, in *The Passions of the Soul*, says this. 'It is certain that we cannot desire anything without perceiving by the same means that we desire it; and although in regard to our soul it is an action to desire something, we may say that it is also one of its passions to perceive that it desires. But . . . this perception and this will are really one and the same thing.' A will, a *volonté*, is for Descartes a particular type of thought or *pensée*. But it is not altogether clear what he means when he says that the will and the perception are the same thing. Is he, as it were, starting from the will, and saying of it that it is also a perception? If so, his claim seems to be that the will is self-luminous, that volition is a type of conscious thought. Or is he starting from the notion of perception, and saying that the way to understand the will is to regard it as a perception of a certain kind? This latter seems more likely: in which case his view is the same as one more clearly put by Hume, when he defined the will as 'the internal impression we feel and are conscious of when we knowingly give rise to any new motion of our body or new perception of our mind'.[1]

The view of the will as an internal impression has never been more clearly expressed than by William James (who was in doubt whether to accept it). James speaks of the way in which a movement (e.g. the utterance of the word 'Peter' rather than the word 'Paul') is guided by the idea of the sensible effects of the

---

[1] Descartes, *Passions*, I, 18–19, Hume, *Treatise*, II, III, 1.

movement ('the very thought of my voice falling on my ear, and of certain muscular feelings in my tongue, lips, and larynx'). He asks 'Is the bare idea of a movement's sensible effects its sufficient mental cue, or must there be an additional mental antecedent, in the shape of a fiat, decision, consent, volitional mandate, or other synonymous phenomenon of consciousness before the movement can follow?'[2]

On the introvert view the will is a phenomenon, an episode in one's mental history, an item of introspective consciousness. Volition is a mental event whose occurrence makes the difference between voluntary and involuntary actions. For an overt action to be voluntary is for it to be preceded and caused by a characteristic internal impression or conscious thought.

The contrasted, extrovert view starts with the observable behaviour of agents and asks for the external criteria by which to distinguish between voluntary and involuntary actions. It may see the mark of voluntariness as being a certain style of activity, or, more likely, as simply the absence of certain untoward features which would render the action coerced or the agent misinformed. On this view to say that human beings have wills can only mean that they can perform, because they sometimes do perform, voluntary actions.

Philosophers in the extrovert tradition regard the volitions of the introvert tradition as mythical entities. One of the most powerful chapters of Ryle's *Concept of Mind* is devoted to showing this. Ryle offers two main arguments. First, if volitions were genuine mental events occurring with the frequency which the introvert theory demands, it should be possible for any articulate human being to be able to answer questions about their nature, occurrence, timing, intensity and qualities. But introvert philosophers have been very unforthcoming about the introspectible qualities of volitions, and Ryle has no difficulty in constructing a battery of questions on the topic to which no coherent answers present themselves. Secondly, Ryle employs a regress argument. Volitions are postulated to be that which makes actions voluntary. But not only bodily, but also mental operations may be voluntary. So what of volitions themselves? Are they voluntary or involuntary motions of the mind? If the latter, then how can the actions that issue from them be voluntary? If the former, then

[2] *Principles of Psychology*, II, xxvi.

in accordance with the introvert theory they must themselves proceed from prior volitions, and those from other volitions and so on *ad infinitum*.

Ryle's criticism of the introvert tradition seems to me on this point decisive. Notice, though, that despite the general animus of *The Concept of Mind* against 'ghostly mental happenings' Ryle is not here denying that there are mental events (deliberation, for instance) which genuinely occur in connection with voluntary action. He is only denying that there is some one mental event which *must always* occur to confer voluntariness on action, as the theory of volitions demands. He writes:

> People are frequently in doubt what to do; having considered alternative courses of action, they then, sometimes, select or choose one of these courses. This process of opting for one of a set of alternative courses of action is sometimes said to be what is signified by 'volition'. But this identification will not do, for most voluntary actions do not issue out of conditions or indecisions and are not therefore results of settlements of indecisions. Moreover it is notorious that a person may choose to do something but fail, from weakness of will, to do it; or he may fail to do it because some circumstances arise after the choice is made, preventing the execution of the act chosen. But the theory could not allow that volitions ever fail to result in action, else further executive operations would have to be postulated to account for the fact that sometimes voluntary actions are performed ... The same objections forbid the identification with volitions of such other familiar processes as that of resolving or making up our minds to do something and that of nerving or bracing ourselves to do something.[3]

Ryle is correct in rejecting the volitions of the Descartes-Hume tradition as mythical; but on the other hand mental acts such as deliberating, deciding, resolving and choosing deserve fuller consideration and more whole-hearted recognition in an adequate theory of the human will than they receive in *The Concept of Mind*.

In the previous chapter it was said that the will is a faculty or capacity. Philosophers in the introvert tradition have often been opposed to talk of faculties: for reasons not germane to the

[3] *The Concept of Mind*, 68.

present topic they have questioned the distinction between a capacity and its exercise and jeered at 'occult powers'. Recent philosophers in the extrovert tradition, on the other hand, have insisted on the philosophical importance of distinguishing those verbs which record capacities or dispositions (like 'know' 'believe' 'love') from those which record events or episodes (like 'work out' 'worry' 'ache'). But in itself the distinction between a faculty and its exercise cuts across the distinction between inner and outer events. One can recognize the will as a capacity from either the introvert or the extrovert viewpoint. The will, that is to say, may be regarded as the capacity for voluntary action irrespective of whether 'action' in the relevant sense covers only external behaviour or also mental activities.

It seems that the use of the English word 'voluntary' in philosophy stems from the use of '*voluntarium*' in medieval Latin as a translation of the word '*hekousion*' in Aristotle's *Ethics*. '*Hekousion*' for Aristotle is not a predicate reserved for actions; both what happens around us and what we do can be divided into things which are *hekousia* and *akousia*. If I see a child drowning and don't jump in when I can and should, then, Aristotle would say, the child's drowning, so far as I am concerned, is voluntary, or perhaps rather, is voluntary for me. In English it is more natural to use a verb to report the inaction as an action, and speak of what is voluntary as 'letting the child drown'.

Aristotle's concept of voluntariness, valuable though it is, is not one which can be used without modification to define the capacity which is the will, or to assist in assessing responsibility. Aristotle includes animals and children among voluntary agents, and he is clearly right to do so on the account which he gives of voluntariness. His account is that something is voluntary with respect to a particular agent if there is no compulsion, if there is the appropriate degree of knowledge, and if the originating cause of the situation (the *arche*) is in the agent (NE III 1–2 1109b30–1111a24). This applies often enough in the case of animals: my dog sees a bone, and he runs for it without anyone pushing him: the *arche* is within, it is his desire for the bone. So his action is voluntary, on Aristotle's account; yet we do not attribute freewill to dogs or hold them responsible for their actions.

Aristotle has been praised by extrovert philosophers because he approaches the discussion of will not via introspection but through a consideration of the factors such as compulsion and misinformation which negative voluntariness. But the internal *arche* which plays a part in his account of voluntariness is something psychic rather than physical, and in this he agrees with the introvert tradition. In order to look for his account of specifically human volition we have to make a subdivision within the class of voluntary items in accordance with the different types of *arche* which may be the originating cause in the voluntary agent. If an act is to be voluntary, then the *arche* must be some kind of wanting or appetition (*orexis*); but Aristotle draws a distinction between various kinds of wanting. In the case of the dog running for the bone, the *arche* is *epithumia*, or sense desire: felt desire for sense-gratification. In the case of the considered actions of rational agents other types of wanting must be considered: in particular, in the context of Aristotle's theory, wish (*boulesis*) and choice (*prohairesis*).

Boulesis, unlike *epithumia*, is clearly something which is peculiar to humans, since it can concern remote and universal objects, like the fall of Troy or the gift of immortality. But it seems to be too remote from action to be, by itself, the type of wanting that we are interested in when discussing human freedom of the will. Its effect on action is via deliberation (*bouleusis*) and choice (*prohairesis*): these are the crucial concepts in Aristotle's account of human agency.

In Book III of the *Nicomachean Ethics* (1113a4) we are told that something is chosen if it is decided on by deliberation. Aristotle's general account of deliberation is valuable and will be discussed later. According to Book VI, however, only the outcome of a particular type of deliberation amounts to a choice.

> The origin of conduct—its efficient, not its final, cause—is choice; and the origin of choice is appetition plus means-end reasoning. So without understanding and reasoning on the one hand, and moral character on the other, there is no such thing as choice; for without reasoning and character there is neither welldoing nor its opposite. Reasoning, in itself, moves nothing; only means-end reasoning concerned with conduct . . . for good conduct is the end in view, and that is the object of the appetition. Therefore choice is either appetitive intelligence or ratiocinative appetite. (1139a30 ff.)

It is this capacity to originate action by choice that Aristotle offers as the defining characteristic of human beings. This is an insight of fundamental importance. But why does he regard moral character—which for him involves a concern with conduct as exemplifying an ideal of life—as an essential condition of choice? Why does he regard good conduct (*eupraxia*) as *the* end of wanting (*orexis*)?

The solution seems to be connected with the account Aristotle gives of means-end reasoning in Book I of the NE. At 1094a20 he says that if we choose everything for the sake of something else, then there will be an infinite regress and *orexis* will remain idle and void; and at 1096b16 and 1097b1 he gives lists of things which we choose for their own sakes, namely pleasure, honour, wisdom, sight, virtue and happiness. Taking our cue from this we might suggest the following account. If a man is asked to give a reason for his action he may either explain that the action is a means to some end, or say that he values it for its own sake. In the former case he will be characterizing it as in some way useful, and in the latter case he must be characterizing it as either pleasant or noble (for these, we are told at 2204b32, are the three possible grounds for choice). If the action is characterized as pleasant, then we can ask whether the man has a general policy of pursuing what is pleasant or not. If so, he is an intemperate man, and we have a case of choice accompanied by moral disposition, namely the vice of *akolasia*. If not, then the agent's pursuit of pleasure is not the result of any choice—he gives no reason for pursuing pleasure in the present instance—and so we have neither choice nor moral disposition, and so no counter-example to Aristotle's thesis that where there is choice there is moral character. If the action done is characterized on the other hand not as pleasant but as noble, then he is doing what he does for the sake of virtue, as the brave man does his brave actions for the sake of what is noble (NE 1116a28). Of course an agent in characterizing his action as noble may be mistaken: this would be the case, for instance, of the intemperate man whose idea of the good life is the pursuit of pleasure: Antony, for instance, telling Cleopatra 'The nobleness of life is this.' We are left with the third possibility that the action is performed qua useful, but in that case it is chosen as a means to some other end. Not everything can be chosen as a means to some other end and whenever our reasoning comes to a stop with something which is chosen for its own sake we can once again ask: is it because it is pleasant or because it is noble that this end is pursued?

So understood, Aristotle's doctrine that there is no choice without moral character appears a perfectly intelligible one. But it will follow from it that only a small sub-class of free human actions are 'chosen': only those that are chosen as part of a worked-out plan of life. Most deliberate human actions seem to be neither on the one hand executions of overall plans of life nor, on the other, impulsive motions on the prick of desire. Our everyday conviction that human beings have free will is something quite different from a theory that they can make Aristotelian choices.

Aristotle was surely right to think that the crucial element in specifically human conduct was its connection with reasoning; and his account of practical reasoning, fragmentary though it is, has remained to this day the starting point for discussion of the topic by philosophers and logicians. But his concept of *prohairesis* places excessive emphasis on those practical reasonings whose overarching premiss is a theory of the good life (cf. EE 1, 1218b8–24).

Professor G. E. M. Anscombe has suggested that the weakness in Aristotle's account is a lack of the concept of intention. She draws attention to the discussion in NE VI of the case of an incontinent man who achieves his purpose by calculation (1142b19). 'When he describes this man as calculating cleverly' Professor Anscombe writes, 'he says he will get what he "proposes" (*protithetai*); and this verb expresses a volition, or perhaps rather an intention. Aristotle ought, we may say, to have seen that he was here employing a key concept in the theory of action, but he did not do so; the innocent unnoticeable verb he uses receives no attention from him.'[4]

The neglected topic of intention is indeed fundamental. Having seen that the will cannot be defined as the capacity for voluntary action, or for prohairetic action, shall we then say that it is the capacity for intentional action? Isn't there the same difficulty with intentional action as there is about voluntary action, namely, that it is within the competence of animals? Surely dumb animals often do one thing for the sake of another—the cat pushes the door open to get into the house, for instance—and isn't doing X in order to do Y precisely what acting intentionally is?

Let us examine more closely the differences between the voluntary behaviour of humans and animals. It is beyond doubt that animals act for the sake of goals, and that they may be conscious of their goals, in the quite literal sense they may see or smell what they are after. However, they do not have the long-term or remote and universal goals that human beings may pursue, such as the discovery of truth or the pursuit of riches. It was principally in this respect that Aristotle located the distinction between human and animal appetition (e.g. NE VII 1147b4). But the relation between human and animal activity is not accurately brought out if we say merely that animals, like humans, act to bring about certain goals but that unlike humans they have only limited and immediate goals of a particular kind. There is a more fundamental difference which was very well brought out by St. Thomas Aquinas, who in this respect greatly improved upon Aristotle's account of human willing.

St. Thomas, unlike Aristotle, thinks that the actions of animals are not full-bloodedly voluntary (Ia IIae 6, 3). To explain why, he starts from the definition of voluntariness as involving an internal origin for an action, and a degree of knowledge of the end. He goes on:

> There are two kinds of knowledge of the end, perfect and imperfect. Perfect knowledge of an end involves not merely the apprehension of the object which is the end, but an awareness of it precisely qua end, and of the relationship to it of the means which are directed to it (*ratio finis, et proportio eius quod ordinatur in finem ad ipsum*). Such a knowledge is within the competence only of a rational nature. Imperfect knowledge of the end is mere apprehension of the end without any awareness of its nature as an end or of the relationship of the activity to the end. This type of knowledge is found in dumb animals.

Full-blooded voluntariness, which permits an agent in awareness of an end 'to deliberate about the end and the means, and to pursue it or not to pursue it' accompanies perfect knowledge; imperfect knowledge brings with it only the second-class voluntariness of which animals are capable.

Aquinas is not denying that animals act for the sake of ends:

so, on his view, do inanimate objects (Ia IIae 1, 2). Why then does he say that they do not appreciate the *ratio finis* and the *proportio eius quod ordinatur in finem*? His doctrine may perhaps be justified as follows. When a human being does X in order to do Y, the achieving of Y is his reason for doing X. When an animal does X in order to do Y, he does not do X *for a reason*, even though he is aiming at a goal in doing so. Why not? Because an animal, lacking a language, cannot *give a reason*. And while a rational agent may, on a particular occasion, act for a reason without giving (to himself or to others) any account of the reason, it is only those beings who have the ability to give reasons who have the ability to act for reasons. Humans are rational, reason-giving animals; dumb animals are not and therefore cannot act for reasons. We can thus justify the conclusion that the human will is the capacity for intentional action. But in the light of the discussion we can see that a better, because a less misleading, account is that the human will is the capacity to act for reasons. Intentional action presupposes language in the same way as self-consciousness presupposes language. Animals, lacking language, may yet have simple thoughts: as, a dog may think that there is a bone buried beneath this bush. But, as I argued earlier, unless a dog masters a language he cannot have the thought *that he is thinking that* there is a bone buried beneath this bush. Similarly, he may scratch to get at the bone, and his scratching manifests his desire to get at the bone; but there is nothing within his repertoire to express *that he is scratching because* he wants to get at the bone.

With humans, of course, it is different. When I run to catch a train, my wanting to get a train may be shown by my running. Quite independently of that I can express *that I am running because I want to get the train*; for I can reply to questions about why I am running, or why I ran. This two-tiered possibility of expression is not open to animals who lack language. Thus, in St. Thomas' terms, though a dog may be aware of his end (he smells the bone he is scratching for) and though his action may be caused by his desire for the end (it is because he wants the bone that he is scratching) he does not know the *proportio actus ad finem*. Nor does he know the *ratio finis*: his conduct may show that the gnawing of bones and sleeping by the fire are both among his ends; but there is nothing in his behaviour to express the possession of a common concept under which both these ends fall.

What animals lack, in Aquinas' terminology, is the ability for *intentio*. The Latin word is not as broad in sense as its English equivalent: it refers to the intention *with which* actions are done, not to the intention *to do* something in the future. It is undeniable that animals intend *to do* things in the sense that it is often true of them that unless interfered with they will go on voluntarily to perform various actions. But, if Aquinas is right, they do not act intentionally, intending a goal which is the reason for their actions.

Aquinas' concept of *intentio* (Ia IIae 12, 5)—the rational direction of an activity to an end—fills the lacuna to which we drew attention in the Aristotelian schema: it falls between the Aristotelian notion of *hekousion* (which was too broad to demarcate human willing) and the Aristotelian notion of *prohairesis* (which was too narrow to encompass it).[5]

Human voluntary action, then, for Aquinas, is action that issues from a rational consideration. But what is rational consideration? Aquinas sometimes contrasts deliberate action with action on a sudden and talks as if it must be a time-taking process of deliberation. If this is his considered view, it seems wrong.

The minimum of rational consideration seems to be that an action should issue from a consideration of the act as answering to a certain linguistic description.[6] Thus if someone behind me calls out 'Get out of the way!' and I jump out of the way immediately, it might be said that my action issued from rationality in the minimal sense that it involved an understanding of language beyond the capacity of a dumb animal. However it

[5] Aquinas believed that every human action was for the sake of happiness: wherever we have a chain of means-end reasoning—where an agent does A for the sake of B for the sake of C . . .—the chain must end with happiness as its final term: a goal not freely chosen, but desired by nature (e.g. Ia IIae 5, 8; 1, 6). I have given reasons for thinking that Aquinas' view on happiness is a mistake—a mistake not shared by Aristotle, at least in the *Eudemian Ethics*—in my paper 'Aristotle on Happiness', in *The Anatomy of the Soul*. Despite this mistake, Aquinas expressly said that *intentio* was not concerned only with an ultimate end or overall plan of life. When an agent does A for the sake of B for the sake of happiness it is true of him not only that he intends happiness, but also that he intends B.

[6] Cf. P. T. Geach's paper 'The Will', 6 ff.

might well be contested whether in cases such as these I have a *reason* for acting, and therefore whether the action issues from rational consideration in the appropriate sense. If rational consideration of an act is to include the having of reasons for acting, then more than the ability to recognize an act as falling under a linguistic description is necessary. One must be able to give reasons for the act: which might take the form either of showing the goodness of the act itself, assigning to it its appropriate desirability characterization, or of showing that the act was a means to a desirable end, and therefore as an outcome of *practical reasoning*.

Still, there are countless cases where one does act for reasons and yet acts immediately without deliberation or reflection: as when the physician examining me says 'take a deep breath' and I do so, or when driving a car I take avoiding action in a sudden emergency. If these actions are done for a reason, then there will be a pattern of reasoning which can be exhibited after the event ('I obeyed the doctor because . . .' 'I turned the steering wheel to the right because'). But the reasons which would appear in the later formulation need not have formulated themselves in the agent's consciousness at the time in order to have been his genuine reasons. In theoretical reasoning too, we often draw conclusions from premises without formulating them. Seeing the coat hanging up in the cloakroom we say 'Oh, so John's home' without rehearsing even in imagination under our breath the *modus ponens* 'If John's coat is in the cloakroom, John is at home. But John's coat is in the cloakroom. Ergo . . .'

If the human will is, as St. Thomas thought, essentially a rational appetite, an ability to have reasons for acting and to act for reasons, then an essential element of any theory of the will must be an account of practical reasoning. The nature of practical reasoning, and the similarities and differences between it and theoretical reasoning, have recently been the subject of research and discussion by logicians and philosophers. Little agreement has been reached on anything except the extreme difficulty of the topic: but from whatever angle the topic is approached it seems clear that the relationship between premises and conclusion in practical reasoning is not as tight or as easy to regiment as that between premises and conclusion in theoretical deduction. When we look at a piece of practical reasoning we often apppear to find where the analogy of theoretical reasoning would lead us to expect necessitation, merely contingent and defeasible connections between one step and another.

Aquinas believed that the peculiar contingency of practical reasoning was an essential feature of the human will as we know it. He regarded this contingency as the fundamental ground of the freedom of the will. This insight, I believe, is both correct and profound. But its content needs to be expressed in non-Thomist terms and evaluated in the light of contemporary discussions of the freedom of the will. This cannot be done until, in a later chapter, we have considered the nature of practical reasoning and investigated the sense in which practical premises can justify, without necessitating, practical conclusions.

The theory of the will as rational appetite presents a third way between the extrovert and the introvert tradition from which we started. It is contrasted with each of those traditions, but contains elements which occur in each of them. Like the extrovert tradition the view I have defended defines the will as the capacity for a certain kind of action; like the introvert tradition it defines the kind of action which the will is the capacity to perform as action issuing from a certain kind of *thought* (conceived, though, not as an item of consciousness but as a mental state). Like the extrovert tradition it approaches the nature of the will via the nature of voluntary behaviour; but as the introvert tradition implicitly did, it assigns a very special place to linguistic behaviour, and in particular to the agent's sincere account of what he is doing and why.

This contrast between Aquinas' view and the introvert tradition would be contested by many Thomists: for his doctrine is often presented as if he was an adherent of the Humean theory of volitions as internal impressions. The attribution of this theory to him must rest principally on the distinction which he makes between two kinds of acts of the will. The exercises of the faculty of *voluntas* are divided into two classes: *actus eliciti* and *actus imperati* (Ia IIae, i 1 ad 2; 6, 4c). *Actus eliciti* are such things as enjoying, intending, choosing, deliberating, consenting (Ia IIae, qq 11–15): he describes them as *actus immediati voluntatis* 'unmediated acts of will'. Among *actus imperati* are voluntary motions of the body such as walking and speaking, acts 'commanded by the will' whose execution involves the exercise of some other power (Ia IIae 17).

Such *actus imperati* are clearly acts whose existence will not be denied even by the toughest behaviourist. But does not Aquinas' recognition of *actus eliciti*, unmediated actualizations of the pure will, ally him so definitely with the introvert tradition as to make him vulnerable to the destructive criticisms of Ryle? What are *actus eliciti* if not the mythical volitions of Descartes and Hume?

When Aquinas says that *actus eliciti* are 'unmediated exercises of the will' he is not referring to mythical acts of pure willing; he means merely that when we describe someone as wanting, or intending, or delighting in something we are merely recording the state of his will, not saying anything about his talents, skills or abilities.

The Latin word '*actus*' need not mean any sort of action at all, whether interior or exterior; it is the term for 'actualization' as opposed to 'potentiality'. Being red, being square, being hot, being a statue of Hermes would all be *actus*, and none of those things are momentary events of the kind suggested by the English word 'act'. Aquinas often speaks of an *actus voluntatis* as being an *inclinatio*, a tendency or disposition rather than an episode.[7] And this tendency can be operative without being present to consciousness, as one's desire to reach a destination can govern one's behaviour on a journey without being the object of one's thoughts (Ia IIae, 1, 6 ad 3). So when Aquinas says that all properly human actions must issue from a *voluntas deliberata* (Ia IIae, 1, 1), he does not mean that they must be caused by an event of consciousness. But it was that theory which was the doctrine of volitions exploded by Ryle. All that Aquinas' language commits him to is the truism that if you do something voluntarily you do it because you in some sense *want* to do it.

If the doctrine of *actus eliciti* does not commit St. Thomas to the introvert view of the will, his doctrine equally cannot be summed up in the extrovert formula that the will is the capacity for voluntary behaviour. In the first place, because the management of one's private thoughts is a function of the will, and a highly important one—if not, as Descartes thought, the only really important one. In the second place, because the category of 'voluntary' for St. Thomas as for Aristotle includes much more than a person's actions, whether overt or internal. A negligent

---

[7] E.g. *actus voluntatis nihil est aliud quam inclinatio quaedam procedens ab interiori principio cognoscente*: Ia IIae 6, 4.

quartermaster, he teaches, may voluntarily let a ship sink without any exercise of his will, whether external or internal. He need not do anything to make the ship sink, nor have any desire that the ship should sink: it is enough that there is something which he could and should have done which would have prevented the ship sinking, namely steering it correctly (Ia IIae 6, 3).

Of the items called '*actus eliciti*' by St. Thomas, some seem to be actions in the ordinary sense of clockable voluntary performances: deciding, for instance, or deliberating. Others, like wanting or intending, are not performances but states. Forming an intention, of course, may be a datable event; but an intention, like, say, a friendship or an inflation, is something which may be in existence at a certain time without there having been any moment *at which* it became into being.

However, though the category of *actus eliciti* does not commit Aquinas to the myth of Humean volitions or pure acts of the will, I think that he was misguided in assigning to that category interior actions such as deciding or deliberating. Making up one's mind to do something may be an interior act in the sense that it is something that one can do without anyone but oneself knowing about it; a decision is a topic on which the person deciding can speak with a unique authority. But these actions are in no sense pure acts of the will, exercises of the will and no other faculty. Deliberation involves the use of the imagination as when, in interior monologue, one weighs up the pros and cons of the proposed course of action. The inward passage from premises to conclusion is an exercise of the reason. But deliberation—as Aristotle insisted—arises from, and culminates in, states of the will: a desire for a particular end issues, via deliberation, in a desire for a means. And these originating and culminating 'exercises of the will' are states, dispositions, attitudes, not actions.

It seems therefore, that deliberation, as described by Aristotle and St. Thomas, is not so much an *actus elicitus* as an inner *actus imperatus*. Whatever Aquinas may have thought, it seems that all genuine *actus eliciti*—all 'pure actualizations of the will'—are states, and not actions or clockable events with a beginning, a middle and an end.[8] The nearest to a 'pure act of the will' that

[8] Professor T. Penelhum has pointed out to me that at Ia IIae 6, 4 Aquinas says that an *actus imperatus* can be impeded by outside forces, but not an *actus elicitus*, because it is 'contrary to the notion of the

we can come without falling into nonsense seems to be the *onset* of a volitional attitude. If I hear of a prospective sharp rise in the value of a certain stock, I may be suddenly smitten with a keen desire to purchase some. Here it is clearly the rational and not the sensual appetite that is in play: none the less the desire may have a sudden onset and perhaps a felt history.

It has been necessary to dwell on the nature of *actus eliciti* in order to show that the broadly Thomist position that I am commending is not vulnerable, as the introvert tradition is, to the charge that it generates an infinite regress.

The challenge against volitions was this: either volitions are involuntary motions of the mind, in which case they cannot give rise to voluntary action; or they are voluntary motions of the mind and thus must be preceded by other voluntary motions and so *ad infinitum*.

If it is accepted that volitions are not motions of the mind, but states of the mind, then this challenge can be met. It can be allowed that voluntary action is action issuing from a volition without this having any implication that volitions must be preceded by volitions *ad infinitum*: volition not being itself an action does not fall under the law that all voluntary action is action issuing from a volition.

But if the Thomist theory can avoid this horn of the dilemma, will it not be impaled on the other? Surely volitions, even if states, can be classed as voluntary or non-voluntary; and if they are not classed as voluntary, how can they be the essential prerequisite for voluntary action? The reply to this is twofold. First, the sense in which volitions can be voluntary is that they like other states can be brought about by voluntary action; not that one can produce desires or volitions to order on the spur of the moment, but that one can change the pattern of one's desires and volitions, more or less deliberately, by thinking the right thoughts, keeping the right company, reading the right newspapers and so on. But the more important point is that a volition does not have to be itself a vóluntary state—a state

will's own act that it should be subject to compulsion or violence'. If so, than deliberating should not be listed as an *actus elicitus*; a blow on the head may interrupt my deliberation about the best train to catch just as it may prevent me getting on the train. This point is treated more fully in my forthcoming paper 'Aquinas and the Will', on which I have drawn.

produced or changeable, at will—in order for an act issuing
from it to be a voluntary action. This can be substantiated only
when we have considered in detail the relation between volition
and ability. At this stage, only a misleading summary can be
given. The state of volition to ϕ, as it figures in the theory of
will as rational appetite, includes two related elements: (1) a
rational inclination to ϕ, (2) ability to ϕ or not to ϕ. Clearly, it is
irrelevant to the question whether my ϕing is voluntary whether
the second element is a feature of my own making or is a gift of
nature or luck. Equally with the first feature: the property of
rational inclination which is essential if there is to be freedom
is not that it should be a self-procured inclination, but that it
should be a non-compelling inclination. No doubt there is a sense,
and an important sense, in which a man who has the inclinations
he wants to have is freer than one whose inclinations go against
his own view of the person he wants to be.[9] But this refinement of freedom is not necessary at the basic level of rational
appetite, the level which is concerned with rationality and responsibility.

It is time to turn from *actus eliciti* to *actus imperati*. The term
'*actus imperatus*' invites us to compare the relationship between
willing and acting to the relationship between a command and its
execution. In my book *Action, Emotion and Will* I gave a sketch
of a theory of volition which was based on taking seriously the
analogy between volition and command. The account met many
difficulties, not all of which I was able to resolve. I concluded the
book with these words:

> Aquinas called the relation 'being commanded by the will':
> fully voluntary action was *actus imperatus a voluntate*. This is
> only a metaphor; but I think that it is the right metaphor. The
> relation between Volition and action has throughout our
> account been explained by analogy with the relation between
> a command and its fulfilment. And just as there are cases where
> it is very difficult to decide whether a man does something
> *because* he wants to, so it is sometimes very difficult to

[9] An excellent account of this feature of human freedom, which is
neglected in the present work, is to be found in a number of papers by
Harry G. Frankfurt, especially 'Freedom of the Will and the Concept
of a Person', *Journal of Philosophy*, 1971.

decide whether a man does something *because* he has been commanded to. Our methods of deciding the latter question are our only clue to deciding the former. (p. 239)

In the following chapter I wish to modify and extend the imperatival theory of the will which I sketched in *Action, Emotion and Will.*

III

THE IMPERATIVE THEORY
OF THE WILL

In an obscure passage of the *Tractatus Logico-Philosophicus* (5.542) Wittgenstein suggested that the proper analysis of sentences reporting beliefs would show that in a belief mental elements corresponding to the objects which formed the topic of the belief stood to each other in a certain relation corresponding to the relation in which the objects themselves stood if the belief was correct. Professor Geach, in his book *Mental Acts*, presented a development of this suggestion which freed it from the mysterious ontology of the *Tractatus*. On his theory, a judgement to the effect that things stand in an *n*-termed relation R itself consisted of Ideas standing in an *n*-termed relation ZR. A judgement to the effect that gold is heavier than lead, for example, would consist of an Idea of gold standing in the relation Z (heavier than) to an Idea of lead. Ideas were defined as the exercises of concepts in judgements; 'Z' was to be defined by reference to the verbal expression of a judgement. The judgement itself was to be regarded as a mental utterance, any sentence of the form 'A judged that *p*' being analysable as 'A said in his heart "*p*" '.[1]

In the last chapters of *Action, Emotion and Will* I gave reasons for believing that the Wittgenstein-Geach theory could be extended to reports of acts of the will. The object of volition displays the same complexity as the object of an act of judgement; there are analogies between reports of volition and reports

[1] Geach's theory seems to be a theory of belief rather than of judgement: judgement seems to be the act which (in some cases) *initiates* a state of belief. It is the state rather than its onset that is analysed as a relation between Ideas; but the difference between the two does not affect the essential point of the theory.

of commands, just as there are analogies between reports of judgements and reports of statements; finally concepts are exercised in commands no less than in statements. In the light of this I considered a simple adaptation of Geach's theory which I proposed along the following lines: when A desires that b should stand in the relation R to c, then A's Idea of b stands in the relation WR to A's Idea of c. 'W' in this theory was definable by reference to the verbal expression of a desire: thus a wish to the effect that p were the case could be regarded as a mental utterance of the wish 'Would that p were the case!'

Because of the variety of grammatical constructions used to report and express affective attitudes, I coined an artificial verb 'volit'[2] to report any sort of pro-attitude, so that 'A volits that p' was equivalent to 'Either A hopes that p, or A wants it to be the case that p, or A regrets that not-p or . . .' A restatement of Geach's theory in terms of volition, so defined, makes it able to deal with reports of all those mental attitudes whose expression, like a command, sets a standard by which facts are judged (as opposed to those whose expression, like a statement, is judged by the standard which the facts provide).[3]

I considered at some length a possible objection to such a theory of volition based on an assimilation of the expression of intention to a command. An expression of intention, the objection went, may be a lie, whereas a command or wish cannot be a lie: how then can a report of an intention be regarded as reporting the mental utterance of something like a command or wish? I replied to the objection by drawing attention to the criteria of sincerity for different types of utterance. A statement is insincere if it is not *believed*, whereas a command, an expression of inten-

---

[2] As a noun corresponding to this verb I used 'Volition', with an initial capital to distinguish what I meant from volitions as internal impressions. In the present work I have dropped the capital V, and use an explicit expression such as 'Humean volition' when I have occasion to refer to the mythical internal impression.

[3] The theory finally stated was a little more complicated than that summarized here, in order to take account of the element in common between a command and a statement, the element which Wittgenstein calls a 'sentence-radical'. Geach's theory, and the simple adaptation of it, failed to take account of the distinction between predication and assertion. The above three paragraphs are a highly compressed summary of a theory spelt out more intelligibly in chapters X and XI of *Action, Emotion and Will*.

tion and a wish are insincere if they are not *meant*. This difference between the two criteria of sincerity, I argued, shows the logical kinship between wishes and commands, and justifies regarding the formation of an intention as the mental utterance of a command to oneself.

Mr. D. R. Bell, in a paper 'Imperatives and the Will' (PAS 1965–6, 129 ff.) named this theory 'The Imperative Theory of the Will'. He showed its similarity to the views of Professor R. M. Hare, who had likewise offered to explain the relation of thought to action in practical thinking through the notion of the components of such thinking being imperative in nature. In favour of the theory, he agreed that volitions were like commands in that they caused (non-Humeanly) or explained actions, and that they stood to actions in an internal relation, which was, he truly said, best explained in the following way: 'the description of an action as intended is the same description as the description given of the act that counts as execution of the intention'. Thinking of intention on the model of self-addressed command, he suggested, solved the regress that we are in danger of getting into when we try to find the ultimate material on which the will acts.[4]

However, Bell took the theory to task on two main grounds. First, it pays too little attention to the difference beween commands, orders, wishes and expressions of intention: orders and commands are essentially other-directed while one's intentions relate to oneself. Secondly, both the issuance of orders and obedience to orders are themselves voluntary performances; an account of volition in terms of inner obedience to a self-directed order therefore cannot avoid falling into a vicious regress.

A similar attack has been mounted against the theory by Mr.

---

[4] 'For many voluntary actions and expressions of intention it is the case that what explicitly we will or intend to do is something that can only be brought about by first doing something else which will have what is explicitly willed or intended as a consequence ... Thus to drive one's car involves shifting the gear lever; shifting the gear lever involves moving one's arm; moving one's arm involves ... moving one's what? One's muscles perhaps? Then to move one's muscles involves activating some neural network. Suddenly the inevitable chain disappears into the murky regions of speculative physiology with the consequence, as it has sometimes been put, that we no longer seem at home in our own actions ... Construing intention on the model of self-addressed command seems a good way of avoiding this *impasse*' (loc. cit., p. 138).

D. Pears in his 1964 Academy lecture 'Predicting and Deciding'. Pears stated the theory thus: 'an expression of intention, like "I will do A", may be regarded as a kind of command addressed to oneself, and that the utterance "I intend to do A", when it is a genuine report of a state of mind, is tantamount to the statement "I have said in my heart 'Let me do A' " '.

The theory so formulated, Pears argues, is vulnerable to the objection that it leaves no room for change of mind: may it not be that I once said in my heart 'Let me do A', but that now I have repented and no longer intend to do A?[5] The objection misunderstands the force of the perfect tense in 'I have said'. It surely indicates, as the grammar books say, 'a state continuing up to the present'. Suppose I have promised to take my children to the pantomime, but I have to change my mind because there are no tickets available. Surely I must say not 'I have said I will take you to the pantomime, but there aren't any tickets' but 'I *said* I *would* take you to the pantomime etc.' The 'I *have* said' carries the implication that—as Hare would put it—I still *subscribe* to what I said.

Like Bell, Pears thought the imperative theory of volition made an excessive assimilation of expressions of intention to commands. Indeed from one passage of *Action, Emotion and Will* he drew the conclusion that my thesis was that intention actually was a species of command. The passage in question ran thus:

> There is no reason, therefore, why we should not, as our theory demands, regard an expression of intention as a command uttered to oneself or a wish about oneself. The insincere expression of intention may be regarded as giving oneself an order, in the presence of one's listener, which one does not mean oneself to obey. It is as if a superior, having received a complaint against a subordinate, should summon the subordinate and tell him in the complainer's presence 'Put this matter right', though both superior and subordinate know that the command is not meant seriously and is issued merely to satisfy the complainer. (p. 220)

[5] Hare also, in a defence of the imperative theory (*Practical Inferences*, pp. 44–58), regards the formulation as vulnerable. Pears regarded this as an easily remediable fault in my statement of the theory; Hare regarded it as an unfairness in Pears' account of my views. Pears' quotation was, in fact, quite accurate. (Cf. *Action, Emotion and Will*, 218.)

From that passage the most that could be concluded is that an *expression* of intention is a self-addressed command, not that an intention is a self-addressed command. None the less, I agree that the passage is misleading. It occurred in the course of a reply to the objection that the imperatival theory of intention leaves no room for lying. In the course of my reply I pointed out that the notion of commanding itself left room for insincerity, as in the example given. The type of insincerity which occurs in expressions of intention, on my view, is the same. 'To see this, look at the expression of intention as if it was a self-addressed order' is what I meant; but it was a bad way to put this to say 'The insincere expression of intention may be regarded as giving oneself an order . . .'

The difficulty is not that one cannot give oneself orders: one can. (For example, a commander may give orders by posting a duty rota, on which his own name appears as well as others'.[6]) But the giving of a command or an order and the expression of an intention are quite different speech-acts; different preconditions have to be met for the felicitous performance of such acts. In particular, it seems to be difficult to conceive of an *internal* command to oneself, while there is no difficulty at all in an internalized expression of intention. ('Tomorrow I really *will* get up at 7.15' muttered behind clenched teeth as one winds one's alarm in solitude.)

Because of this difficulty, Pears, in trying before criticizing my theory to present it as sympathetically as possible, substituted self-exhortation for self-addressed command. He explained, in a later paper (in *Agent, Action and Reason*) in which he developed the argument of his Academy lecture:

> My reason [for doing so] was that there are obvious objections to taking commanding to be the speech-act which is, as it were, internalized when 'I will do A' is analyzed as 'Let me do A'. I chose self-exhortation instead, because it seemed to me to be the least inappropriate speech-act for the drama which, according to this version of the theory, would be enacted *in foro interno* every time that a person utters 'I will do A'. (p. 112)

[6] But doesn't this differ from a standard command in that the commander can always let himself off when the time for execution comes? Not necessarily: when that time comes it may be that his orders remain in force even though he has himself ceased to be in command.

Pears then went on to develop a number of objections to treating intention in this way.

The objections to treating intention as self-exhortation are well taken: but the implausible identification of internal speech-acts which is attacked is no part of the imperative theory of volition. The essence of that theory was that there were a large number of *different* speech acts, and different mental acts also, which had in common that their appropriate form of expression had the features of the imperative *mood*. The imperative mood, even in its natural uses, is not restricted to any single type of speech act: it is used in requests, prayers, exhortations, instructions and advice as well as in commands and orders. My suggestion that, for the sake of perspicuous and uniform analysis of reports of volitions, one might make use of *oratio recta* reports of the mental utterance of first-person imperatives was intended as an artificial extension and exploitation of this feature of natural usage. The artificial expression of an intention in the imperative form 'Let me do A' no more equates intending with commanding than the use of the imperative in 'Give us this day our daily bread' turns the Lord's prayer into an order to God. My use of a single form of analysis for all volitional attitudes is simply parallel to the customary philosophical use of 'belief' as the mental counterpart of stating, claiming, conjecturing, admitting and a host of other assertoric speech-acts.

Even after this misunderstanding has been cleared away, however, one objection of Pears' remains. The primary purpose of the utterance 'I will do A' and 'I intend to do A' is, he maintains, to convey information, but this is not the primary purpose of any self-addressed utterance in the imperative mood. I agree that 'I will do A' and 'I intend to do A' may be used to give information as well as to express an intention and that it may sometimes be difficult to tell which of the two a speaker is doing and that sometimes he may be doing both at once. My claim is only that in so far as 'I will do A' is an expression of intention it can be expressed in a philosophically less misleading way as 'Let me do A'; and in so far as it is a genuine report, it is tantamount, on the imperative theory, to 'I have said in my heart "Let me do A" '.[7]

[7] Here I am happy gratefully to accept the defence of my view against Pears made by Hare on p. 56 of his paper.

There is therefore no foundation for the argument of Bell and Pears that the imperative theory of the will involves a confusion of speech acts. Bell's argument that it involves a vicious regress has in effect been dealt with in the discussion of Aquinas' *actus eliciti* in the previous chapter. For volitions are not mental performances but *states*; so that from the thesis that every voluntary action must issue from a volition it does not follow that every volition must proceed from another volition and so on *ad infinitum*. Some volitions are themselves indirectly voluntary, and others are not: the desire for food, for instance, is normally not voluntary in its onset, but may be if I take a run for the purpose of working up an appetite before a banquet. An intention may be involuntarily manifested or voluntarily expressed; whether it is so or not has nothing to do with whether what gets expressed or manifested is a volition.

To remove a final misunderstanding of the imperatival theory, I should emphasize a point made in several places in *Action, Emotion and Will* that the artificial notion of 'saying in the heart' does not involve the attribution of silent monologue speech or, in Hare's words, 'subvocal mouthings' to the person whose mental state is being reported. Volition may be expressed aloud, or in a *sotto voce* aside, or in the inner theatre of the imagination. It may indeed fail to be expressed in any of these ways: provided that volition to do A is truly attributed to a human being, then he has said in his heart 'Let me do A'. For to say 'He has said in his heart "Let me do A" ' is simply to say 'He is in a mental state expressible as "Let me do A" '.

Rather than develop further any reply to the criticisms of the imperative theory of the will, I propose for the remainder of this chapter to restate its philosophical aspects from a fresh start. The rationale of the theory is the fact that mental states are identified by their expression. Volitions are no exception: the way to understand volition is to study the nature of its expression.

In recent philosophy, the systematic study of the difference between the verbal expression of belief and the verbal expression of volition began with Frege's introduction into logic of a special 'assertion sign'. Frege's distinction between predication and assertion is highly important: unfortunately, its value has been obscured by the unclarity of Frege's account of the assertion sign's purpose.

Three quite different functions are attributed to the sign. Sometimes the assertion sign is considered as a sign that what follows it is seriously meant, that is to say, that it is meant to be taken seriously and not as part of a charade or fiction. Secondly, it is taken as marking the beginning of the sentence, or more generally, as distinguishing a complete sentence from a subordinate clause occurring within a sentence. Thirdly, it is taken as being the mark of the assertoric mood, when it is said that its function is to distinguish an assertion from a supposition or a question.

Frege treats the assertion sign as a sign that what follows is seriously meant when he says that in fiction we are only interested in the sense of sentences and not in their truth-values whereas judgement of which the assertion sign is the mark, is an advance from a thought to a truth-value. Actors on the stage, he says, utter words which are signs having only a sense; the assertion sign, which is used to assert that the reference of what follows it is the true, cannot be used in conjunction with signs which have no reference, and therefore cannot be used by an actor on the stage. (*Philosophical Writings*, 63–5; 156.)

Against *this* function of the assertion sign Wittgenstein protested that it was a mistake to think that 'assertion consists of two actions, entertaining and asserting (assigning the truth-value, or something of the kind) and that in performing these actions we follow the propositional sign roughly as we sing from the musical score'.[8] Now though not every proposition which is asserted is first entertained, entertaining and asserting are in fact quite different actions which are separable: as Frege says, a hypothesis may have been in one's mind for years before one is prepared to assert it as the truth. Meaning a sentence is certainly not like singing from a score: one does not mean first one word and then another, as one sings first one note and then another. Nor is meaning as it were an extra note which is sung before or after the notes which constitute what is meant.

One might think, in the context of this image, that it was more plausible to regard the assertion sign as like a key signature; or better, as like a treble clef. Just as the clef shows how each note follows it is to be read, so, we might think, the assertion sign

---

[8] *Philosophical Investigations*, I, 22.

shows that each word following it is to be taken seriously. And this seems to be what Frege meant.

But it is obvious that a sign to denote that a sentence was to be taken seriously would be quite futile. If it was in question whether an ordinary sentence was to be taken seriously, it could equally be questioned whether a sentence preceded by an assertion sign was to be taken seriously. I am not fortified against having my leg pulled by your prefacing your remarks with 'Seriously'. Frege himself said that if an actor on the stage uttered the sentence 'the thought that 5 is a prime number is true' he would no more have made a serious assertion than if he said '5 is a prime number'. But it is equally obvious that an actor who in the course of a play wrote an assertion sign on a blackboard would not be thereby making a serious judgement either.[9]

Whether an utterance is meant seriously is quite different from the question whether the utterance is a complete unit of sense and from the question whether the utterance is in the assertoric mood or in some other mood. Perhaps it is true that only a complete sentence, or an utterance which can be plausibly represented as an ellipsis for a complete sentence, can be seriously meant. If I say 'The life of man' the question whether I meant it seriously or not does not so far arise. But a sentence can be complete without being asserted in the seriously-meant sense: as the majority of sentences in the *Odyssey* and Shakespeare's tragedies. Again, the question: 'Did you mean that seriously?' can arise about commands no less than about statements. Indeed, it can also arise in the case of mere suppositions, which are Frege's favourite example of utterances which are *not* assertions. If I say 'suppose that *Fanny Hill* was written by John Wesley' this may be meant just as a joke or an example; or it might be meant seriously as a hypothesis which it might be worth the trouble to verify.

With this we can leave the first of the three possible functions of the assertion sign. We are left with two: to mark the beginning of a sentence, and to usher in the assertoric mood. (I am using the word 'mood' to mark the distinction between assertoric and imperative sentences. Some grammars talk also of the indicative and subjunctive moods: this is a distinction which arises within the assertoric.) In its actual use Frege's sign always does both of these things together; but it is clear that the two functions are

[9] Cf. Anscombe, *An Introduction to Wittgenstein's Tractatus*, 113.

separable. Wittgenstein says (loc. cit.): 'It distinguishes the whole period from a clause within the period. If I hear someone say "it's raining" but do not know whether I have heard the beginning and end of the period, so far this sentence does not serve to tell me anything.' Obviously the same point could be made about the imperative. If I hear the words 'put on your coat' but do not know if I've heard the beginning and end of the sentence, then for all I know what was said was 'If it rains either put on your coat or take an umbrella.'

It is the third use, as a mark of mood, which corresponds to the traditional use of 'assertion' in contrast to command and question. In spite of some dismissive remarks of Wittgenstein about this division I think that it is of fundamental importance. But the division calls for two comments.

First, assertion and command may be thought of as two different kinds of sentence, or two different speech-acts. The same speech act can be performed by different sentences, and the same sentence may be used in different speech-acts. ('Mary will show you to your room' may be used to give information to you and an order to Mary.) In the manner explained earlier in this chapter, volitions correspond rather to sentences than to speech-acts.

Second, if the division between assertoric and imperative sentences is to be exhaustive, assertoric sentences will have to include many which would not normally be thought of as assertions, and imperative sentences will have to include many which would not commonly be called 'commands'. Suppositions and guesses will have to be ranked with assertions, and requests, wishes and questions must go with commands. This lumping together can be justified. To do so we must take account of something which was called by J. L. Austin 'onus of match'. Any sentence whatever can be regarded as—*inter alia*—a description of a state of affairs—provided the sentence is not meaningless or self-contradictory. Which state of affairs it describes is settled by the conventions governing the sense, and the context determining the reference, of the expressions contained in the sentence. Now let us suppose that the possible state of affairs described in the sentence does not, in fact, obtain. Do we fault the sentence, or do we fault the facts? If the former, then we shall call the sentence assertoric; if the latter, let us call it for the moment imperative.

Thus, a wish about the past 'if only you hadn't done that' will count as a command, since it is the past action (your doing it) which I am faulting for not according with my wishes. No doubt it seems artificial to call a wish about the past a command, and only slightly less so to call it an imperative sentence. Let us therefore adopt an artificial term 'fiat' (proposed by Hofstadter and McKinsey in an article of 1939, 'The Logic of Imperatives') for sentences that come out imperative on the test of onus of match. Commands proper are then a subclass of fiats: commands and requests are called in this terminology 'directives'. Any sentence in the optative mood, in any tense, will be a fiat; for instance 'Please God he'll come', 'if only you were here', 'would I had never been born'. A directive is a fiat uttered to an agent: it gives the agent to understand that he is to realize the fiat. The giving of commands, and the making of requests, are speech acts which are made by means of directives. Commands and requests are also fiats: all directives are fiats, but not all fiats are directives. The notion of a directive is more complicated than that of a fiat. For a fiat to be satisfied, it suffices that the state of affairs described in it should obtain. For a directive, the state of affairs must be brought about by the agency of the person to whom the *because of* the utterance of the directive.

Whereas directives are commonly second-person sentences and can be issued only in a single tense, the future, fiats can be uttered in all tenses and persons. Some verbs, like 'can' and 'want', have no grammatical imperative for use in directives. But any verb which can occur in an assertoric sentence can occur in a fiat. Fiats, unlike directives, display a perfect parallelism with assertoric sentences. To use Hare's terminology, to each assertoric sentence, there corresponds a fiat which can be analysed as having the same phrastic as the assertoric sentence and as differing from it only in the tropic.[10] We could read the tropics indeed, as 'Est' and 'Fiat'; 'please', *pace* Hare, goes rather with directives. I shall write '𝕰p' and '𝕱p' for Est-p, and Fiat-p.

[10] To bring out the relationship between the command 'Arrive on Wednesday' and the prediction 'You will arrive on Wednesday' Hare, in *The Language of Morals*, analysed the former as 'Your arriving on Wednesday, please' and the latter as 'Your arriving on Wednesday, yes'. The common element ('Your arriving on Wednesday') he called 'the phrastic'; the 'yes' and the 'please' which mark the difference between indicative and imperative he then called the 'neustic' but now the 'tropic'

Fiats and assertoric sentences, whether written with the resources of natural language, or broken up artificially into phrastics and tropics, are linguistic expressions. They have in common those properties which belong to their phrastics. ℭp and ℑp do not differ in meaning, in the sense in which meaning is equivalent to sense plus reference and is fixed by convention and context. They are sentences with different moods but the same descriptive content.

Both fiats and assertoric sentences can be looked on as expressions of states of mind. An assertion may be the expression of a belief, a fiat the expression of a volition. This must not be misunderstood. To issue a command or to give utterance to a wish is not to report a desire: fiats are not psychological statements. But to express a volition is not the same as to report a volition. An assertion, similarly, does not report a belief. But it may be the expression of a belief. Of course, an assertion may be a lie. In that case it expresses a belief which the utterer does not have. Fiats too can express volitions which the utterer does not have.

The psychological item corresponding to assertion is sometimes called judgement. Perhaps it is more accurate to say that a judgement is the formation of a belief, belief being the state which results from the act of judgement. But not all beliefs are preceded by judgements. There is not, I think, any general expression for the formation of a volition to correspond with the notion of making a judgement; though 'make up your mind' may cover both. But among fiats we must include expressions of intention. Intentions are often the results of decisions. In that case, intention appears to be related to decision as belief is to judgement. Just as not all beliefs are the result of judgements, so not all intentions are preceded by decisions.

Mental acts and states of minds, I said earlier, can be identified by their expression. Many mental states are too complicated to be expressed whether by an assertion or by a fiat alone. Emotions, for instance, are rarely simply volitions and never simply beliefs. But many of them can be expressed by some combination of assertion and fiat, with the addition of modal and tense-operators to the phrastic. Using Fp and Pp for the future and past tenses corresponding to p, we might make the following crude approximations.

$Ⅎp$ plus $Ⅎp$ expresses pleasure that p
$ⒺFp$ plus $ℲFp$ expresses hope that p
$ⒺFp$ plus $ℲNFp$ expresses fear that p
$Ⓔp$ plus $ℲNp$ expresses regret that p.

Is there anything which stands to volition as knowledge stands to belief? An interesting suggestion about this is to be found in Russell's *The Philosophy of Logical Atomism* (pp. 216 ff.). (Russell uses 'desire' as I use 'want' or 'volit' and 'volition' as the analogue for knowledge.)

> I am inclined to think that volition differs from desire logically in a way strictly analogous to that in which perception differs from belief.

It may be that by 'volition' Russell meant a mythical mental event of the kind canvassed by Hume. But the context here suggests not. Russell was discussing what he called 'propositions with two verbs' and he was interested in the contrast between believing and perceiving which is illustrated by the fact that from 'A perceives that p', but not from 'A believes that p' one can infer 'p'. It seems, then, that he had in mind a sense of 'will' in which from 'A wills that p' one could infer 'p'; this would be contrasted with 'A desires that p' from which it does not follow that p. 'Volition' in Russell's sense would then be effective volition; the volition which is effected in voluntary action.

Russell's suggestion would of course give odd results if applied to the word 'will'; in ordinary English if somebody wills that p it does not follow that p. But there are English phrases involving the concept of willing which exhibit the characteristic in question. 'A ϕd of his own will' and 'A ϕd willingly' both imply 'A ϕd'. There are good reasons for the use of an adverbial phrase rather than a separate verb. But let us, for the moment, adopt Russell's suggestion and construe 'A wills that p' as 'A willingly makes it the case that p'. 'Will' so interpreted will be quite analogous to 'perceive'. With some oversimplification we might present the analogy as follows.

'A perceives that p' entails   (1) p
(2) A believes that p
(3) A's belief that p derives in a special way from the fact that p.

'A wills that p' entails   (1) p

(2) A volits that p

(3) The fact that p derives in a special way from A's desire that p.

Obviously, enormous difficulties lurk here: the phrase 'derives in a special way' covers up all the problems concerning the causal theory of perception. But it seems clear enough that in a full explanation of how it came about that I saw that the cat was on the mat, the fact that the cat was on the mat would have to be mentioned; and if it is of my doing (of my voluntary doing) that the cat is on the mat, then my desire for this state of affairs would have to be mentioned in a full explanation of how the cat came to be there.

Does the parallel continue to hold in the case of knowledge which is not perceptual knowledge? There does not seem to be any quasi-causal relationship between the fact that 2 and 2 are 4 and my knowledge that 2 and 2 are 4, whatever some philosophers may have thought. But that does not mean that the parallel breaks down. For it seems that the truths of arithmetic can be learnt only by the artful manipulation of symbols; and similarly, there are wishes that can only be expressed by symbolic behaviour. A dog cannot wish that Troy had not fallen, or that $\sqrt{2}$ were not incommensurable any more than it can know that $7 + 5 = 12$.

Much of our knowledge derives not from our own perception, but from the testimony of others. Similarly, much of what we effect in the world we bring about not by own action, but through commands and requests to others. For our knowledge of what happened before we were born we must rely very greatly on testimony: similarly, to give effect to our wishes after we die we must entrust them to executors. We must, in the significant phrase, make our will. So the parallel suggested by Russell can be pursued surprisingly far.

Cognitive	Affective
Assertion	Fiat
Believe	Volit
Judge	Decide

Perceive	Will
Knowledge *a priori*	Idle wishing
Testimony	Command

If we prolong the 'cognitive' column, of course, sooner or later we must put in 'inference'. Can we write it in the 'affective' column also? Some philosophers would perhaps deny this. At least they have denied that there is such a thing as imperative inference; but perhaps no one would wish to deny that there is such a thing as practical reasoning; and this surely belongs in our 'affective' column. Practical reasoning, it appears to me, can very well be looked at as a process of passing from one fiat to another according to rules, just as theoretical reasoning consists in passing from one assertoric sentence to another according to rules. The point of the rules for theoretical reasoning is to ensure that one never passes from true assertions to false assertions. We shall consider in a later chapter what is the point of the rules for practical reasoning.

Since Bolzano logicians have spoken not only of sentences—linguistic expressions—but also of propositions. A proposition in this sense is something thinkable or expressible but not necessarily thought or expressed; something which can be expressed variously in various languages and which whether expressed or not is capable of truth and falsity. In this sense of 'proposition' there are many propositions which nobody has ever judged or believed and which yet are either true or false. One element, that is to say, in this concept of proposition is the abstraction of the content of a judgement from any particular judger.

Is there any affective analogy of a proposition? Is there anything which stands to desires and fiats as propositions stand to beliefs and assertoric sentences? We might argue as follows. One and the same wish may be expressed in fiats in several different languages, or not expressed at all; and one and the same state of affairs will gratify the wish thus variously expressed or unexpressed. Thus far, it seems, the parallel holds; and we might introduce the term 'optation' to match 'proposition'. We might use the term to speak of the common features of actual or possible utterances that resemble each other completely as vehicles of communication in the imperative mood.

Such an optation would be, perhaps, an odd sort of entity: a wish, as it were, that is nobody's wish. But is it any odder than a proposition, if that is a belief which is nobody's belief? We might argue thus. When we say that the proposition that p is true, we mean that if anyone believes, or says that p, then he believes or says truly. The 'if . . . then' here is not the truth-functional connective: we do not mean 'if anyone says that the moon is made of corned beef, he says truly' to be true simply on the grounds that nobody says the moon is made of corned beef. We mean that though nobody does in fact believe this, if he believed it he would believe truly. The oddity of the proposition, it may be argued, is simply the oddity of modality and the counterfactual. And this— we know from other fields—we have to live with. So too with optation. We may say that the optation that there should be 2,345 hairs on my head is gratified. In saying this we do not mean that anyone has ever uttered the fiat or felt the desire that there should be 2,345 hairs on my head, but that if anyone had done so his fiat and his wish would have been gratified. Altogether then: there may be difficulties in the notion of optation, but whatever difficulties there are arise also for propositions.

But in fact there is no need to think of optation as distinct from proposition. Both correspond to the *content* of a speech-act; and this is the same in both the assertoric and the imperative case.

When we attribute wants to agents there are two elements in our attribution: there is the optation (the content of the want) and the location of the optation (*whose* want is in question). A candidate expression of volition has to be identified as the voluntary action of the willer if it is to be a genuine expression of volition. Words written by my hand do not express my desires if my hand was in the irresistible grip of another; if Cardinal Mindszenty at his trial was merely uttering words like a ventriloquist's doll then they did not express *his* remorse for his alleged crimes against the state. So the linguistic expression of wants is in one way parasitic on the non-linguistic manifestation of wants. Words of mine which merely coincided with my wishes would not be an expression of my wants unless uttered for that purpose.

We seem here to be in danger of proceeding in a circle. Human voluntary action is action in accordance with the agent's volition. An agent's volition is identified by his expression of his volition. But nothing can be an expression of a volition unless it is a voluntary action. How then can the occurrence of volition and voluntary action ever be detected? In the following chapter we must consider how the notion of voluntary action must be related to other notions, such as those of need and power, if we are to be able to identify voluntary action as such independently of the ascription of volitions whose expression is linguistic.

IV

VOLUNTARINESS AND INTENTIONALITY

Voluntary actions are a subclass of a very much wider genus. Agency is a universal phenomenon; and though it may be human agency which interests us most, it is absurdly provincial to restrict the application of the concept to human beings or even to living beings. Many of the very same verbs of action which we use of humans apply also to animals: 'eat', 'hug', 'fight', 'pull', 'build', 'migrate' and a host of others. Animal agency is undeniable: but animals are not the only non-human agents. The grass pushing its way between the crazy paving, the Venus' fly-trap closing on its prey, the action of *aqua regia* on gold or of hydrochloric acid on litmus paper—all these are examples of action by non-conscious agents. As the examples show, such action may or may not be teleological in the sense of being aimed at the good of the agent.

It is not always easy to identify genuine agency in the inanimate case: in particular it is often difficult to demarcate the exact agent. Are fire and rust agents, or the wind and the sea? Is a crystal an agent? Is an electron? The answers given to such questions as these may change with the progress of science: but the very fact that with hindsight we can see that some ancient answers to these questions were *wrong* answers shows that we have here a concept which admits of application to the inanimate world. Wherever we can talk of substances in nature, wherever we can talk of natural kinds, we can talk also of natural agency and natural powers.

The concepts of agency and power are obviously connected: the natural actions of an agent are exercises of its natural powers. When we are discussing conscious agents, in the explanation of their actions we must take account not only of their powers, but also of their knowledge and their goals. In studying the activity of any living organism we are interested in its repertoire of behaviour, in its acquisition of information, and in its characteristic goals: that is, in its capacities, its cognitive and volitional functions; in its power, its intellingence, and its desires. If we observe the behaviour of an animal and have knowledge of any two of these factors, we can often infer the third. Given knowledge of an animal's capacities and of the information available to it, we infer its goals from its behaviour: we know which foods dogs like by watching which foods they take from among those they can sense which are within their reach. If we want to study the perceptual discrimination of animals we set them a task within their known capacities (e.g. pressing a bar) which will lead to one of their known goals (e.g. food): from capacity and goal we infer cognitive state. If we want to test their ability to perform tasks, we provide them with information about means to their known goals: we show them the bananas on the tree and a pair of sticks and see what they do. In general, you cannot infer what an animal wants from what he does unless you also know how much he knows and what he is capable of; nor can you infer his state of knowledge or belief unless you know his wants and his repertoire of behaviour.

In human beings power, intellect and will form a related triad: the connectedness between the three elements of power, intellect and will comes out in many ways. One manifestation, which is familiar to philosophers, is the problem of weakness of will, which arises when a man says that he ought not to ϕ, but none the less ϕs. Three types of solution to this problem have been explored by philosophers. They may say (with Socrates, and perhaps Mill) that he does not really *know* that he ought not to ϕ, or that he is ϕing. Or they may say (with Aquinas and Ross) that he does not really *want* to do what he ought. Or they may say (with perhaps Augustine, and certainly Hare) that in some profound sense he *can*not refrain from ϕing. Later, we shall take a side in this debate; notice for now that the breakdown between profession and practice is explained either as a failure of intellect, of will, or of power.

The notions of consciousness, voluntary behaviour, and desire are closely linked to each other: they become applicable together when the behaviour of an agency manifests a certain degree of complexity. Professor Anscombe writes in her book *Intention*:

> The primitive sign of wanting is trying to get; which of course can only be ascribed to creatures endowed with sensation. Thus it is not mere movement or stretching out towards something, but this on the part of a creature that can be said to know the thing. On the other hand, knowledge itself cannot be described independently of volition; the ascription of sensible knowledge and volition go together . . . one cannot describe a creature as having the power of sensation without also describing it as doing things in accordance with preconceived sensible differences. (*Intention*, 67)

The actual behaviour of an animal is the resultant of desire and belief. As we remarked, to test what faculties an organism has, you set it goals, and try what tasks and what discrimination it can perform to achieve those goals; to find what goals it pursues you set various objects within the range of its senses and find which it chooses. This procedure, it seems, may lead to a methodological breakdown: how can you ever tell what the beliefs or goals of an animal are? For given any probable goal which an animal pursues, you can reject the hypothesis that it is pursuing that goal by attributing to it a sufficiently bizarre system of belief; given any probable belief of an animal, you can reject the hypothesis that it holds that belief by attributing it to a particularly perverse set of goals.

It seems that the way to break into this charmed circle is to make use of the notion of need.

Need is a very important concept comparatively little studied by philosophers; and I cannot pretend to have an adequate account of it. As a first approximation we may say that an agent A, has at a given time t a need for something X if A lacks x at t, and A cannot continue to survive (or survive as a good specimen of its species) unless A comes to possess X. This is clearly excessively schematic, and applies only to the most basic type of need: it does not account for why we speak of needing things for a particular purpose. But it will serve for our present requirements: for in this context the important thing about the notion of need is that we can decide what something's needs are without observing its behaviour.

Indeed, we can assign needs to things which do not, in the full sense, 'behave' at all. Nonsentient things like plants have needs: flowers need water if they are not to die. Even non-living things have needs, though perhaps only by a zoomorphic extension of the term: it is quite natural to speak of the fields needing rain (if they are to produce a good crop) and my car needing a new clutch (if it is to continue functioning).

There seems here to be a hierarchy extending upwards from stones through plants and animals to men; from no needs, through needs and then desires, to volition and will. There are as usual borderline cases: is it correct to say that fire needs oxygen in order to burn?

When we assign wants to animals, we make the assumption that they want what they need. Why do we not make the same assumption with plants? There seem to be two reasons. If we are to assign wants to an agent, the agent must have available to it a number of different ways of getting its needs. Not only that, but the agent must also exercise the activities in its need-satisfying repertoire in cases where there is no need. (Animals and plants both feed; but only animals play.) Moreover, at least in the case of those animals with whom we feel most at home in attributing wants, the choice of exercise of the repertoire is connected with variations in the stimulation affecting particular parts of the body which can therefore be identified as sense-organs.

Some languages have a special word for the type of desire which belongs to animals: Aristotle called it '*epithumia*'. Human beings, of course, share such desires, and in their early years have no others: only as reason develops is room made for volition alongside desire.

Epithumia or sensual desire differs from volition, *inter alia*, by its relation to sensation: it is *felt* desire, and it is desire for something *now*, desire which is more or less continuously felt until it is satisfied (like hunger, sleepiness, thirst). Another difference, according to Aristotle, is that sensual desires, unlike volitions, are not contradictorily opposed to each other: one can simultaneously want that p and want that not p, but not both of these wants can be *felt*.[1]

Aquinas, working in the Aristotelian tradition, defined sensual

[1] This appears to stand in need of qualification to make it precise (cannot hunger and nausea be felt simultaneously?).

desire (*concupiscentia*) as a tendency arising from sense-perception (cf. Ia, 8c, and 8b). This definition seems too broad: if a connoisseur or a miser sees a silver bowl in a silversmith's window and covets it, his desire arises from sense-perception (the sight of the bowl) and yet it may be a highly intellectual desire. Perhaps we should say that the tendency arising from the sense-perception must be a desire for sense-gratification: desire to *go on gazing at* the silver bowl, by contrast with desire to *possess* the silver bowl, may well be sense-desire or *epithumia*.

Desire is not just consciousness of need; I may be conscious of a need I have without desiring to satisfy it or feeling the desire to satisfy it—amphetamines for instance may take away the desire, though not the need, to sleep. Consciousness of bodily needs without the desire-tendencies would be like the consciousness of a sailor of the needs of his ship—a consciousness which Descartes rightly said was not a good analogy for the mind's consciousness of the body's needs. Desire is not even just the feeling of need; it has to be a feeling leading in general to appropriate action. It is conceivable that felt need might be like felt aches: it might just cause one to hug oneself and lie immobile.

Desire cannot be identified with the sensations characteristic of particular desires because desire, unlike sensation, has an internal relationship to action. The internal relationship between desire and action is similar to the internal relationship between volition and action. Consequently it will become clearer when, having offered an account of practical reasoning, we are in a better position to spell out what is meant by saying that an agent did an action *because* he wanted to.

But can it be said that desire is related to action in the same way as volition is? Surely, in what we have said so far, volition and desire have been identified in two totally disconnected ways. 'Volition' was introduced as an abstract term of art to refer to mental states whose expression in language had certain semantic or pragmatic features. 'Desire' on the other hand has been interpreted in the narrow sense of *epithumia* and the concept has been demarcated in terms of its relationship to need, behaviour, and sensation. The internal relationship between volition and action is easy to see: for the mental state which is the volition to act in a certain way is identified by its expression which in its turn contains a description of the action to be performed. What analogue of this is there in the case of desire? Desire surely does not contain a description of its object; we are happy to attribute desires to agents to whom we do not attribute language.

The answer to this is that though wants do not presuppose language, they do presuppose recognitional capacities: we cannot attribute desire to an agent which cannot recognize things as answering to its desires. When we attribute desires to animals we do make use of the same forms of *oratio obliqua* as we do in reporting the wants of human beings: we say, for instance, that the dog wants his master to open the door for him. In using such language we need not be so anthropomorphic as to believe that the animal possesses our concepts of 'master', 'door', 'open', and so on; we need only mean that the dog has a repertoire of concepts, one of which picks out the object we pick out by our concept 'master', another of which picks out the object we pick out by our concept 'door'; and yet another picks out the action we pick out by 'open'. This point has been well made by Professor Armstrong, who points out that what we have here is only an extreme case of the opacity which affects our use of language when we apply *oratio obliqua* in the ordinary way to human beings also.[2]

There is nothing anthropomorphic in attributing concepts to animals; anthropomorphism comes in only if we attribute to them concepts whose possession cannot be manifested by recognition and non-verbal reaction, and which require for their expression the possession of a symbolic apparatus (e.g. the concepts of numbers or of logical constants, or of abstractions like space, time and necessity).

Because the attribution of any sort of wanting involves the attribution of recognitional capacities, there is a feature in common between desire and volition which entitles us to regard them both as a species of the genus *want*. The difference between them is that volition involves the exercise of concepts which need language for their expression, whereas desire need involve only the exercise of simpler and more rudimentary concepts, which can be manifested in non-linguistic behaviour. Of course in order to report—and even to express, rather than manifest (cf. Anscombe, *Intention*, sections 1 ff.)—a desire, we need to make use of language, of language which might be used to express a

[2] *Belief, Truth and Knowledge*, 113.

volition: in this sense our characterization of the desires of non-language users has to be roundabout, taking a route through the analogy with our own volitions.

Just as the needs of animals form the orienteering point for the assignation of desires, so the needs and desires of human beings form the orienteering point for the understanding of the linguistic expression of volition—the needs and desires that we share with other human beings and to some extent with animals. This is why Wittgenstein said that if a lion could speak we would not understand him: we would not understand the language of a race whose needs and desires we shared in no way.

In the case of adult human beings even the desires of the kinds we share with animals are coloured and modified by our possession of language: as my hunger becomes progressively more uncomfortable I keep thinking 'still an hour to go before dinner', using concepts that are well beyond the competence of a hungry dog. Thus, for much of our human affective experience there is a degree of artificial regimentation in drawing a line between desire and volition. The nearest we can come in our own experience to pure animal desire is the case of inarticulate striving to a particular goal from which deviations can be sensed: as when, learning to ride a bicycle, I constantly react by appropriate or inappropriate bodily activity to the tugs and jolts that show I am losing my balance, without being able to give any description in language of the movements with which I strive to recover equilibrium.

Because animals have wants, there is clearly a sense in which it is appropriate to attribute voluntary action to them: for one of the most natural definitions of 'voluntary action' is 'action done because the agent wants to do it'. Aristotle, as we remarked earlier, regarded animals as voluntary agents, and he was surely right to do so.

Voluntary action is also naturally thought of as action which is done in the presence of open alternatives. In the most obvious sense animals seem to have this capacity too—if it is indeed a different capacity. When I call him, my dog *can* come home if he wants to; but if he wants rather more to follow up that interesting smell leading to the cowshed, he can do that too.

This two-way ability also was something which interested Aristotle, who drew a sharp distinction between rational powers, such as the ability to speak Greek, and natural powers like the power of fire to burn. If all the necessary conditions for the exercise of a natural power were present, then, he maintained, the power was necessarily exercised: put the wood, appropriately dry, on the fire, and the fire will burn it; there are no two ways about it. Rational powers, however, are essentially, he argued, two-way powers, powers which can be exercised at will: a rational agent, presented with all the necessary external conditions for exercising a power, may choose not to do so. A skilled Germanist at the podium of a hall filled with sharp-eared German speakers may for reasons of his own refuse to speak or may launch into ancient Gaelic. (*Metaphysics*, *Theta*, 1046a–1048a.)

Aristotle was surely wrong to identify rational powers and two-way powers. If someone speaks a language I know in my hearing it isn't in my power not to understand it; and on the other hand, animals without reason have two-way abilities and exercise choices. It is not at the level of voluntariness, but at the level of intentionality that the distinction between men and animals is to be drawn.

Intentional actions appear to be a subclass of voluntary conscious actions. Not all actions of human beings are conscious: snoring, for instance, is commonly not conscious. Not all conscious human actions are voluntary: reflex actions such as blinking under stimulation are conscious but involuntary. Voluntary conscious actions, it seems, are conscious actions over which we have control. There are, of course, degrees of control; and so we might say that there are degrees of voluntariness. Breathing, for instance, is not completely voluntary, but admits of some degree of control. I can't choose whether to breathe or not, *simpliciter*; but I can hold my breath, and breathe in when the doctor tells me to. The nature of control is obscure. I leave this difficult topic unexamined. But henceforth, in discussing human actions, I shall have in mind voluntary actions. Some conscious voluntary actions are unintentional. They are those actions which one does not do on purpose, and which can be inhibited with an effort. Examples would be wincing in pain, fidgeting, sneezing, laughing, using an irritable tone of voice, mentally brooding over an injury. Intentional actions are distinguished from other conscious voluntary actions in virtue of the agent's state of mind with regard to the results and consequences of his actions.

In *Action, Emotion and Will* I distinguished between *performances*, the bringing about of states of affairs in the world (e.g. killing a man, baking a cake, opening a door), and *activities* which go on for an indefinite time and have no particular terminus (e.g. running, laughing).[3] Substantially the same distinction has been made by von Wright as a distinction between *act* which is the effecting of a change, and *activity* which keeps a process going.[4] I adopt his terminology, and following him I shall make a distinction between the result and the consequence of an act.

The result of an act is the end state of the change by which the act is defined. When the world changes in a certain way there may follow certain other changes, perhaps by natural necessity. In that case we may say that the second transformation is a consequence of the first and of the act which brought the first about. The relation between an act and its result is an intrinsic relation, and that between an act and its consequence is a causal relation.

The consequence of one act may be the result of another and the activity involved in the two may be identical. For instance, the consequence of the act of opening the window may be that the room becomes cooler; but the room's becoming cooler is the result and not the consequence of the act of cooling the room; but it may be by one and the same activity—e.g. movements of my hand—that I both open the window and cool the room. Von Wright says: 'One and the same change or state of affairs can be both the result and a consequence of an action. What makes it the one or the other depends upon the agent's intention in acting, and upon other circumstances which we shall not discuss.' This could be misleading in two ways. In the first place, one and the same state of affairs cannot be the result and a consequence of one and the same act: it either is or is not the state of affairs by which the act is defined. Nor can one and the same state of affairs be both the result and the consequence of an activity: for an activity has no result in the sense defined by von Wright. In the second place, the distinction which von Wright draws between result and consequence applies to inanimate as

---

[3] *Action, Emotion and Will* (1963), 171–86.
[4] *The Varieties of Goodness* (1963), 115–17; *Norm and Action* (1963), 39–42.

well as to animate agents, and therefore can be made without any appeal to intention.

Let X be the movement of a body which brings about the state of affairs that p. Let p and q describe the state of affairs in some close relation to each other such that q is the case because p is the case. Let A be the act of bringing it about that p, and B the act of bringing it about that q. An agent who brings it about that p in such a case will also bring it about that q. In doing A he will also do B; his movement X will be describable as A or as B. In order to apply von Wright's distinction between result and consequence we must restrict the pattern to cases where the connection between p's being the case and q's being the case is causal and not logical. Then we can say: that p is the result of A, and that q is a consequence of A, and that q the result of B. If there was a logical connection between the results then there would be a logical connection between act A and its consequence, which goes counter to von Wright's definitions.

The pattern we have sketched is fundamental to the description of intentional action. But it applies also to non-human and human non-intentional action: for instance, a falling tile, by piercing the skull of a passer-by, may cause his death. Doing B by doing A is not necessarily intentionally doing either A or B.[5]

Over and above this interlocking hierarchical structure which applies to actions of both animate and inanimate agents there are further factors to be considered when we consider the voluntary actions of conscious agents and the intentional actions of human agents. These factors are the wants and beliefs of the agent: in the human case, the volitions and information which provide the reason for action. These concern, *inter alia*, the agent's own actions, both before and during their performance, and combine with the general structure of action thus far considered to yield the pattern of means and ends. If the agent described above wants it to be the case that q (wants to do B) and does A in order to do B, then he knows that he is doing B by

[5] The possibility of giving different act-descriptions of the same movement in such a way that the consequence of one act appears as the result of another is called by Feinberg and Davidson 'the accordion effect' For no clear reason, Davidson wishes to restrict the accordion effect to the actions of intentional agents. ('Agency', in *Agent, Action and Reason.* 17.)

doing A and he wants to do B. He may or may not want to do A for its own sake or as a means to some other end.

The concepts of means and ends define what it is to act intentionally. An agent intends an action if he (a) knows he is doing it and (b) does it because he wants to do it for its own sake or in order to further some other end. If an agent wants to do something as a means to an end, he wants it because it answers to a certain pattern of practical reasoning: if he wants it for its own sake then he regards it as answering to a description which characterizes it as inherently desirable. The immediate satisfaction of desire by a non-rational animal is not in the same way action 'done for its own sake' or 'done as an end in itself'; for to choose something as an end in itself is to choose it as answering to a particular type of rational consideration, not to choose it in surroundings where reason does not come into play at all.

What it is to be a means and what it is to be an end can itself be explained in terms of the general structure of action plus volition and cognition: and it is this structure which provides the pattern which is adopted in practical reasoning, as we shall see in greater detail in the next chapter. When a rational agent wants it to be the case that q and not in order to make anything else the case, we may say that q is his ultimate end. If he knowingly brings it about that q by bringing it about that p, then we may say that p is his means to that end; if A is the act of bringing it about that p, then it is also natural to call A a means of bringing it about that p; and we can also call it a method of B-ing. That p, which is the result of A, we may say is a step towards the end (that q); and that q, which was the result of B, we may say is a consequence of A. An action may be both a means to an end, and an end in itself.[6]

I have stated that a man intends the ends he sets himself and the means he adopts to those ends. This theory can be expanded by the following theses.

    i One intends the result of any act one does intentionally.
    ii One foresees the result of any act one does knowingly.

[6] An action may be an end in itself without its result being an end: if I jump over a fence for fun, being on the other side of the fence, though the result of the act of jumping over, is not an end in itself. An end which is not a means to any other end is an ultimate end; otherwise it is an intermediate end. Cf. Taylor, *The Explanation of Behaviour*, 28.

iii One may do an act knowingly without intending its result, if one does it without wanting it as a means or an end.

iv If one does an act intentionally, and its result is the consequence of the result of another act, then in doing that other act, one intends its consequence.

v If one does an act with a certain result in order to bring about a consequence of that result, then one also does the act of which the consequence in question is the result.

vi One may do an act whose result is the consequence of the result of another act, without doing that other act in order to perform the act first mentioned.

These theses leave open the following question: does one intend the foreseen consequences of one's ultimate end? Let us first suppose that these consequences are themselves wanted. It might be thought that this case could not arise: if the consequences are wanted must they not themselves be a further end beyond the ultimate end, which is absurd? This is not so unless the consequences are wanted enough to be brought about in any case independently of the end of which they are consequences. The case in point is where the agent reasons: 'I want q so I will bring it about that p; but if q then r will be the case also; but r is welcome so I will bring it about that p all the more willingly'. Even in such a case it would seem to me wrong to say that the consequences were intended, since they do not form part of the chain of practical reasoning which leads to the initial decision to bring it about that p. If this is so, then a fortiori consequences which are foreseen but which the agent is indifferent to or regrets are not intended. Of course, it may well be correct to hold the agent responsible for these consequences, but that only means that we can be held responsible for more than we intend.

Besides consequences we sometimes have to consider concomitant effects or side effects of people's actions. Let me explain the distinction. If A is bringing it about that p and B is bringing it about that q, and if p then q, and if q then r, then r is a consequence of both A and B. But in a case where we do not have if q then r, but if p then r, then r while a consequence of p is an effect which accompanies q and which we might call a concomitant of bringing it about that q. For instance, if I open the window to look out of it, and by opening the window cool the room, then the cooling of the room is a consequence of the opening of the window but a concomitant and not a consequence of my looking out of the window. We may explain the notion of a side effect as follows. If r is a concomitant of q and q is a means to s, then r will be a side effect of the action which is bringing about that s. For instance, noise is a side effect of fast travel in a motor car because it is a concomitant of the operation of the engine which is a means to the speed of travel. Concomitants, or side effects, of an end or an action may themselves be both foreseen and desired and adopted as ends: as in cases of killing two birds with one stone. Unless this is the case, however, it seems to me that they are no more intentional than consequences, with one exception to be made in the case of side effects. The exception depends on the distinction between necessary and chosen means. If there is only one means of achieving the agent's purpose then these are necessary means, but if the agent believes that there is more than one way of achieving his purpose then the means he adopts are chosen means. If he chooses a means which has a certain side effect knowing and wanting this side effect, then it seems that he intends this side effect, if that is his reason for choosing this means rather than another, even though he would never have performed the action at all were it not a means to his original purpose.

The unintentional bringing about of foreseen consequences and concomitant and side effects of intentional actions is itself a form of voluntary action: such actions indeed, along with the purposeless but inhibitable actions like yawning and brooding which we mentioned earlier, seem to exhaust the class of unintentional but voluntary action in human beings. If an action is to be voluntary at all, then it must be in some sense done because it is wanted: but if it is to be unintentional then it must be neither wanted for its own sake nor as a means to any further end. The sense of 'want' in which all voluntary actions are wanted actions is a minimal one: to say that an agent wants to ϕ in this sense is merely to say that he knows that it is in his power to refrain from ϕing if only he will give up one of his chosen purposes. It is perhaps misleading to say that in such a case the agent wants to ϕ at all: it might be clearer to say that he ϕs voluntarily because his ϕing is the result of his volitional state: but it is not his wanting to ϕ which is the relevant volition, but his wanting to do something else, for which φing is the price he must (perhaps unhappily) pay. The wanting in question is the wanting of willingness or *consent*: consent, we know, is something which may be accompanied with varying degrees of enthusiasm diminishing to reluctance and nausea. We can thus say that all voluntary action must be action which is performed willingly in the sense that it must be accompanied with at least consent: but if not intentional it need not be accompanied by any other sort of wanting.

The concept of intention which I have presented, with the distinction I have drawn between intentionality and voluntariness, is I believe a coherent one. It also resembles fairly closely the ordinary man's intuitions about what acts to describe as intended or done intentionally.[7] There is, however, another concept of intention which is probably more widely accepted among professionals in several fields, according to which all the foreseen consequences of one's voluntary actions are intentional, whether or not aimed at as ends or means. The most authoritative proponent of that view was Jeremy Bentham, who drew, within the realm of intention, a distinction between direct and oblique intention, which resembles the distinction I have drawn between intentionality and voluntariness.[8]

Because of the resemblance between the distinction Bentham drew and the one I have drawn it might be thought that the question whether to call foreseen but undesired consequences 'intentional' was merely a matter of terminology. If philosophical usage were entirely insulated from non-philosophical usage that might be so. But the concept of intention is one which is used in a systematic way not only by philosophers but also by all those concerned with the assignment of responsibility, from judges to social workers. To see how confusion of terminology and lack of conceptual clarity in this area can have serious practical consequences it is instructive to look in some detail at the history of some recent decisions concerning malice aforethought in the English law of murder.

The maxim of common law *actus non facit reum nisi mens sit rea* insists that no act can be criminal unless accompanied by a

---

[7] The correspondence is not exact: see my paper 'Intention and Purpose in Law' in Summers, *Essays in Legal Philosophy* (1968), 146–66, on which parts of this chapter are based.

[8] *Principles of Morals and Legislation*, ch. VIII.

certain mental state. But the state of mind which constitutes *mens rea* varies from crime to crime. Let us suppose that the law wishes to prohibit a certain action, which it describes without reference to the agent's state of mind (e.g. using a motor vehicle uninsured). The law may wish this *actus reus* to be punishable (1) no matter whether the agent did know or could have known he was doing it; (2) no matter whether he did know, but only if he could have known he was doing it; (3) no matter whether he wanted to do it, but only if he knew or thought likely that he was doing it; (4) only if he wanted to do it, either for its own sake, or for some unspecified further purpose; (5) only if he wanted to do it for some further purpose specified in the law.

In the first case, there is no *mens rea* at all, and the law will be one of strict liability: such is the English statute forbidding the sale of adulterated milk. In the second case, the crime will be one of negligence: negligence resulting in death constitutes one species of the common law crime of manslaughter.

The law distinguishes between direct and oblique intention in cases which come under the fifth head above. A criminal intention may make an innocent act criminal (e.g. loitering with intent) or make an offence more serious (e.g. wounding with intent to kill carries a severer penalty than simple wounding). In such cases, oblique intention is insufficient: for instance, one does not commit the crime of doing an act likely to assist the enemy with the intention of assisting the enemy if the assistance to the enemy is merely foreseen and in no way desired (R. v. Steane (1947), K.B. 997). Similarly, to commit the crime of attempted murder, one must act *in order to* kill, and not simply act foreseeing death as a likely outcome.

In the case of murder, it is the second, third and fourth cases which come into consideration.

Murder, in English law, is killing 'with malice aforethought' but in the words of a distinguished contemporary lawyer 'there is no doubt that neither the word "malice" nor the word "afore-thought" is to be construed in any ordinary sense' (Cairns, L.J. in Hyam's case before the Court of Criminal Appeal). Clearly, if A kills B because he wants to kill B as an end in itself or as a means to some further end, that is murder. But suppose that he doesn't in this way directly intend to kill B, but only to injure him. Is that still murder? Suppose that the death (or injury) of B isn't something he wants as an end or a means, but something he simply foresees as the upshot of action he is taking for some other purpose. Is that still murder?

For a long period the answer which English law has given to both these questions has been 'Yes'. In the case of R. v. Desmond (1868) a Fenian conspirator was found guilty of murder because, by dynamiting the wall of Clerkenwell prison to liberate two imprisoned fellow-conspirators, he had caused the deaths of persons living near by. In summing up, Lord Coleridge said 'It is murder if a man did an act not with the purpose of taking life but with the knowledge or belief that life was likely to be sacrificed.'[9] In R. v. Vickers (1957), Lord Goddard reaffirming a rule which some thought had been abolished by the Homicide Act of 1957, defined murder as killing 'with the intention either to kill or to do some grievous bodily harm'. (Quoting from the trial judge (1957), 2 Q.B. 664, 672.)

Clearly the effect of these two decisions extends the definition of murder well beyond cases of killing with the express purpose of killing. The definition was widened even further in 1962 in connection with the case of D.P.P. v. Smith (A.C. 190). Smith was driving a car containing stolen property when a policeman told him to draw into the kerb. Instead he accelerated and the constable clung to the side of the car. The car zigzagged and collided with four oncoming cars; the policeman fell off in front of the fourth and was killed. Smith drove on for 200 yards, dumped the stolen property, and then returned. He was charged with murder and convicted by the jury. He appealed to the Court of Criminal Appeal which quashed the conviction and substituted one for manslaughter. The Crown took a further appeal to the House of Lords, which restored the conviction for murder.

It was never suggested that Smith intended to kill the policeman, but it was contended that he intended to do him grievous bodily harm, on the grounds that a reasonable man must have foreseen that such harm was likely to result from his actions. The

[9] Decisions such as this are taken by some lawyers to show that foresight is a form of *mens rea* alternative to intention to murder, by others as showing that the concept of intent to be applied in murder is the Benthamite one (e.g. *Salmond on Jurisprudence*, 12th edn., p. 370, 'Thus if I do an act which I know is very likely to kill Smith and he dies as a result, I cannot be heard to say that I did not intend his death').

decision of the House of Lords made the long traditional presumption that a man intends the natural consequences of his acts into an irrebuttable one. The Lord Chancellor, giving judgement in the House of Lords, said

> The jury must . . . in such a case as the present make up their minds on the evidence whether the accused was unlawfully and voluntarily doing something to someone . . . Once . . . the jury are satisfied as to that, it matters not what the accused in fact contemplated as the probable result or whether he ever contemplated at all, provided he was in law responsible and accountable for his actions . . .

The natural way to read this is that to be guilty of murder the accused need not himself foresee grievous bodily harm (much less directly intend it, or intend or foresee death): it is enough that a reasonable man would have foreseen it.

Many lawyers criticized the decision in Smith for thus, as they put it, substituting an objective test of malice aforethought in murder for a subjective one. A reform of the law was suggested in a report of the Law Commission (1967). This suggested that no court or jury should be bound to infer that a man intended or foresaw the natural and probable consequence of his actions. It also recommended that killing should not amount to murder unless done with intent to kill; a man has such an intent 'if he means his actions to kill, or if he is willing for his actions, though meant for another purpose, to kill in accomplishing that purpose'.

The first but not the second of these recommendations was embodied in the Criminal Justice Act of 1967. If the second recommendation had been accepted death which was obliquely intentional would still count as murder: for if one fails to desist from a course of action one knows is likely to cause death, then one is willing for one's actions to kill in accomplishing one's purposes: this is the minimum form of willingness which in our previous discussion we called 'consent'. The Law Commission's proposal, therefore, fell short of its avowed aim of bringing legal terminology into accord with ordinary language. For ordinarily a man would be said to intend his actions only when their result is not only foreseen but wanted as a means or end. Thus, a man who rises in the night for a drink of water may know that he will wake the baby without intending to wake the baby.

Because the Criminal Justice Act of 1967 accepted only one half of the recommendation by which the Law Commission hoped to undo the undesirable effects of the Smith decision, it left the definition of murder in a confused state. A 1974 case (R. v. Hyam) gave the House of Lords an opportunity to clarify this confusion (H.L. (E), W.L.R. May 10, 1974, 698 ff.). The accused in this case was a woman who had had a relationship with a man who became engaged to be married to B. In the early hours of the morning she went to B's house and poured petrol through the letter box, stuffed newspaper through and lit it. She gave B no warning but went home leaving the house burning. B escaped from the house but her two daughters were suffocated by the fumes of the fire and the accused was charged with their murder. Her defence was that she had set fire to the house only in order to frighten B so that she would leave the neighbourhood. The jury were directed by the trial judge to concentrate on the intent to do serious bodily harm, and told that the prosecution had proved the necessary intent if the jury were satisfied that when she had set fire to the house she had known it was highly probable that the fire would cause such harm. The jury convicted, and the accused's appeal against conviction was dismissed by the Court of Appeal.

By a majority of three to two, the House of Lords dismissed the appeal. The reasons given by the majority judges appealed to three different theories of the malice aforethought required for murder, and it is of considerable philosophical interest to follow their arguments (W.L.R. May 10, 1974, 608 ff.).

Lord Hailsham addressed himself first to the question whether an intention short of the intention to kill was sufficient for malice aforethought. The Homicide Act of 1957, he maintained, had recognized as a form of malice aforethought a state called 'implied malice' which was rightly taken in *Vickers* to be the intention to do some grievous bodily harm. Parliament in 1967 in enacting the first and failing to enact the second of the two draft clauses of the Law Commission had shown that while rejecting an objective criterion for intent, it wished to retain the intention to cause grievous bodily harm as a possible alternative to intent to kill as the essential mental element in the crime of murder.

No degree of foresight, Hailsham maintained, was sufficient to constitute the required *mens rea*. Intention was necessary. Intention could not be identified with motive, in either of two senses of that word: (a) emotion prompting an act, in the present case the appellant's jealousy of B, (b) purpose, end, or object. 'Intention', he said, 'embraces, in addition to the end, all the necessary consequences of an action including the means to the end and any consequences intended along with the end.' This definition, it can be seen, is close to the one argued for earlier in this chapter.[10]

At this point it becomes more difficult to follow Lord Hailsham's argument. He drew from the case he had so far presented the reasonable conclusion that the question 'does a knowledge that it is highly probable that one's act will result in death or serious bodily harm suffice for malice aforethought?' must be answered in the negative. In the case in point, moreover, as he said, the most that could be said is that 'what was intended was to expose the inhabitants of the house to the serious risk of death or grievous bodily harm and not actually to cause death or grievous bodily harm'. He did not agree that *Desmond* showed conclusively that foresight, while not constituting intent, was an alternative species of malice aforethought. None the less he went on to qualify, indeed almost to reverse, the negative answer to the question of public importance on which the case turned. He argued as follows.

> What are we to say of the state of mind of a defendant who knows that a proposed course of conduct exposes a third party to a serious risk of death or grievous bodily harm, *without actually intending those consequences*, but nevertheless and without lawful excuse deliberately pursues that course of conduct regardless whether the consequences to his potential victim take place or not? In that case, if my analysis be correct, there is not merely actual foresight of the probable consequences *but actual intention to expose his victim to the risk* of those consequences whether they in fact occur or not. (p. 620, italics mine)

This distinction between the intention to bring it about that *p* and the intention to bring about the risk that *p* brings a great

[10] Though, with respect, there is the possibility of confusion in talking of means as consequences, and a certain circularity in singling out *intended* consequences.

deal of light into this difficult area. On the test proposed wherever the intention to bring it about that p is sufficient for murder if death results the intention to bring about the risk that p should also be sufficient.

Unfortunately, Hailsham does not make it clear whether he is applying in the case of the intention to bring about a risk the same careful distinction between foresight and intention as he does in the case of the intention to bring about death or grievous bodily harm. In his final summing up he says that murder must be an act committed with one or other of three intentions, of which the third is

> Where the defendant knows that there is a serious risk that death or grievous bodily harm will ensue from his acts, and commits those acts deliberately and without lawful excuse, the intention to expose a potential victim to that risk as the result of those acts.

On the basis of this principle, he dismissed the appeal.

It is not clear either in the enunciation of the principle or its application to the case whether the intention is meant to be an extra factor supervening on the knowledge, deliberation, and lack of justification of the acts, or whether the presence of those three elements is itself taken to *constitute* the third species of intention. But let us suppose that we follow consistently the definition of intention offered earlier in this chapter, with which the first part of Hailsham's speech appeared to be in accord, and say that the creation of the risk is intended only if the creation of the risk was an end or a means to an end. There would, on the facts of the case, be no difficulty in concluding that the creation of the risk of grievous bodily harm was in fact intentional; as the appellant herself said, she wanted to frighten B into moving away from the neighbourhood; the way she chose to frighten her was to put her and her family at serious risk.

But if we imagine the facts of the case slightly altered, an equally risky action might not have been intentional. Suppose that in order to vent her hatred of B she had stolen all the love-letters and keepsakes exchanged between B and her own former paramour and set them alight in B's doorway with petrol; and suppose that the house had burnt down as before and the children been killed. I do not find it easy to discover from Hailsham's speech

whether he would wish his test to be applied in such a way that
on those altered facts the appellant would have been found guilty
of murder. Consistent with his earlier view, it seems, he should
not have wished in these cases a guilty verdict to be brought
in; but he has been taken by a number of authorities to have
meant that foresight of the very probable result of grievous
bodily harm was enough to constitute intent and thereby malice
aforethought.

One thing that is quite clear in Hailsham's judgement was
that he regards the intent to bring about a risk of grievous bodily
harm as amounting to malice aforethought no less than the
intent to bring about a risk of death; and no doubt in practice it
would often be difficult to distinguish the two. Lord Diplock,
however, thought that *Vickers* and *Smith* were wrong in allowing
the intent to do grievous bodily harm as an alternative: they
should have accepted the submission that in order to amount to
the crime of murder the offender, if he did not intend to kill,
must have intended or foreseen as a likely consequence of his act
that human life would be endangered. The decisions in those cases,
he argued learnedly, were based on a misreading of the history
of the doctrine of constructive malice from Lord Ellenborough's
Act of 1893 (which made it a felony to wound people with intent
to do them grievous bodily harm), right up to the Homicide Act
of 1957 (which abolished the doctrine of constructive malice
which had made it murder to kill in furtherance of a felony).
The House of Lords should now overrule *Vickers* and *Smith* and
take the opportunity, which had been lost in those cases, to restrict the relevant intention on a charge of murder to an intention
to kill or to cause a bodily injury known to be likely to endanger
life. The appeal should therefore be allowed. In this conclusion
he was followed by Lord Kilbrandon.

On the nature of the state of mind denoted by 'intent' Diplock
said

> ... no distinction is to be drawn in English law between
> the state of mind of one who does an act because he desires it
> to produce a particular evil consequence, and the state of
> mind of one who does the act knowing full well that it is likely
> to produce that consequence although it may not be the object
> he was seeking to achieve by doing the act. What is common
> to both these states of mind is willingness to produce the par-

ticular evil consequence: and this, in my view, is the *mens rea* needed . . .

This 'willingness' is what we earlier called 'consent'. To allow it to be enough to constitute intention is in effect to make all intention oblique intention, to equate intention with foresight. Lord Hailsham was well advised to resist this equation.

However, the two judges who supported the Lord Chancellor in rejecting the appeal both agreed with Lord Diplock against him on the nature of the state of mind constituting *mens rea* for murder. Lord Dilhorne cited the authorities for equating intent with foresight, and those for regarding foresight as an alternative form of malice aforethought, and concluded

> Whether or not it be that the doing of the act with the knowledge that certain consequences are highly probable is to be taken as establishing the intent, I think it is clear that for at least 100 years such knowledge has been regarded as amounting to malice aforethought.

For his own part, he sided with those who equated foresight with intent. Lord Cross of Chelsea distinguished between a logician's sense of intention which could not be equated with foresight and an ordinary man's notion of intention, according to which no more than some degree of foresight was necessary—surely an IRA car bomber intends to injure those who are hurt when his bomb explodes! Both the broad and the narrower sense were sufficient to constitute malice aforethought.

Neither Lord Dilhorne nor Lord Cross was prepared without further argument to follow Lord Diplock in excluding grievous bodily harm as a possible alternative content to a murderous intent, and accordingly they dismissed the appeal.

To the layman it seems a pity that the House of Lords did not combine the insights of both Lord Hailsham and Lord Diplock and define the *mens rea* required for murder as being the direct intention to kill or to create a serious risk of death. If, as Lords Diplock and Kilbrandon believed, and as Lord Cross of Chelsea professed himself willing to believe, it was open to the court to reverse both *Vickers* and *Smith*, then in restricting the content of murderous intent to killing and endangering life the House would have made the law of murder take the form which, in the opinion of all of them, and of all who have tried to codify the English law of homicide, it *ought* to take. And in restricting the nature of the *mens rea* to direct intention instead of allowing it to embrace foresight they would have brought greater conceptual clarity into the law and brought legal terminology more closely to common parlance.

Lord Hailsham was particularly concerned that the *mens rea* for murder should not be defined in such a way that a surgeon operating in a case of high risk should not fall under the definition. On the definition I have suggested this danger would clearly be avoided; the creation of a risk to the patient's life is no part of the doctor's plan, it is not a means or an end for him; and any technique which will alleviate that risk he will welcome. As Lord Hailsham himself well says early in his discussion

> The surgeon in a heart transplant operation may intend to save his patient's life, but he foresees as a high degree of probability that he will cause his death, which he neither intends nor desires, since he regards the operation not as a means to killing his patient, but as the best, and possibly the only, means of ensuring his survival.

But later he says that the reason why the heart surgeon, exposing his patient to the risk, is not guilty is because he is 'not exposing his patient to the risk without lawful excuse or regardless of the consequences'. This move seems both unnecessary and dangerous. It is unnecessary because once it is recognized that the surgeon does not directly intend the risk to the patient's life, there is no need to ask whether he has an excuse or not. It is dangerous because if it is admitted that there can be a lawful excuse for intentionally creating a risk of life, the question must be raised what such excuses are and how far they extend: and Lord Hailsham—in marked contrast with the erudition he displayed on the topic of intent—did not feel it necessary, or did not find himself able, to quote a single case on the topic.

In the particular case of Hyam it is perhaps not easy to settle whether she was intentionally creating a risk to life or only intentionally creating a risk of serious bodily harm. But it does not seem to be an objection to the definition suggested that it makes this case into a borderline one: it looks as if the majority of the House thought that it *ought not* to come within the definition of murder, though a majority of them thought it did so. The other cases which preoccupied their Lordships, namely terrorist bombings, would commonly not be difficult to bring under the definition suggested: the paradigm case of terrorist bombing is where the bombing is in order to spread terror precisely by creating widespread risk to life and limb. Where the creation of risk to life is not part of the plan—as may be shown, for instance, by the nature of precautions taken, or the particular placing of the bomb —then surely death which may result *should* not be taken as murder.

This long excursus into recent legal history has had as its purpose to illustrate the practical importance of conceptual clarity on the topic of intention. The concept of intention which has been recommended depends essentially on the notion of the choice of means and ends. An understanding of these concepts in their turn depends on an exploration of the concept of practical reasoning.

V

PRACTICAL REASONING AND RATIONAL APPETITE

It is beyond doubt that in addition to theoretical reasoning there is practical reasoning. We work out, with the aid of logic, not only what is the case but also what we ought to do. In practical reasoning as in theoretical we pass from premises to conclusion. The premises, perhaps, set out our desires or our duties; they set out also the facts of the case and the possibilities open; the conclusions are actions or plans of action. But what are the rules by which we pass from premises to conclusion? What are the criteria for validity in practical inference? It is by no means easy to say.

Consider the following simple piece of practical reasoning:

I'm to be in London at 4.15
If I catch the 2.30 I'll be in London at 4.15
So I'll catch the 2.30.[1]

Reasonings of this form—which we might call the *modus ponens* of practical reasoning—are as ubiquitous (and as unlikely to be stated in artificial articulateness) as their counterparts in normal theoretical *modus ponens*. Clearly in some sense we use a different logic, or use logic in a different way, when we reason practically and when we reason theoretically. For in the ordinary logic used in theoretical reasoning 'q. If p then q. So p' is not a valid argument form, but the fallacy of affirming the consequent.

Some may object that it is not a valid form of argument in practical reasoning either, because it does not necessitate its conclusion. Surely I don't *have* to catch the 2.30; I could as well

---

[1] 'I'm to be' in the premiss is not meant to express any obligation; the premiss is intended as a colloquial equivalent to 'Fiat (my being in London at 4.15)'.

catch the 1.15. Accordingly, some writers have commended systems of practical inference in which conclusions drawn must always concern *necessary* means to some end.[2]

I think that this is an impoverishment of the scope of practical reasoning. It is true that if I am to be in London at 4.15, and I have the information that if I get the 2.30 I'll be in London at 4.15, and if I catch the 1.15 I'll be in London at 4.15, then 'I'll catch the 2.30' isn't the *only* conclusion I can draw. But even theoretical reasoning doesn't necessitate its conclusion in *this* sense. If I know that p, and that if p then q and r, I don't *have* to draw the conclusion that q; or even any conclusion at all.

The necessity of theoretical reasoning is this: that if the premisses are true and the argument valid, the conclusion cannot but be true. For the rules of theoretical reasoning are designed precisely to ensure that we do not pass from true premisses to a false conclusion: they are truth-preserving rules. Now if we are to ask in what sense practical reasoning necessitates its conclusion, we must ask: what is the value which rules of practical reasoning have as their purpose to preserve in the way in which truth is the value preserved by rules of theoretical reasoning?

In looking for an answer to this question it is instructive to follow the discussion in Aristotle, who was the first, and is still the most illuminating, philosopher to write on practical reasoning.

Discussing deliberation in NE III, Aristotle writes:

> We deliberate not about ends but about means. For a doctor does not deliberate whether he shall heal, nor an orator whether he shall persuade, nor a statesman whether he shall produce law and order, nor does any one else deliberate about his end. They assume the end and consider how and by what means it is to be attained; and if it seems to be produced by several means they consider by which it is most easily and best produced, while if it is achieved by one only they consider how it will be achieved by this and by what means *this* will be achieved till they come to the first cause, which in the order of discovery is last ... And if we come on an impossibility, we give up the search, e.g. if we need money and this cannot be got; but if a thing appears possible we try to do it. (1112b18 ff., trs. Ross)

[2] Cf. G. H. von Wright, in *Acta Sociologica*, 1972.

Making use of an example which Aristotle gives in a relevant passage of the *Metaphysics*, we might set out an example of such deliberation as follows:

> This man is to be healed
> If his humours are balanced, he will be healed
> If he is heated, his humours will be balanced
> If he is rubbed, he will be heated
> So I'll rub him.   (1032b19)

Here the balancing of the humours is the necessary means to health; rubbing and heating are means to this; and rubbing is not impossible, but is in the doctor's power; so he begins his treatment by this, which was the last thing to occur in his practical reasoning.

Practical reasoning of this kind we might call propositional practical reasoning: it is done in terms of 'if's and 'then's, and if formalized would look like a bit of deduction based on the propositional calculus ('S; Iff R, then S; if Q then R; if P then Q; so P'). Most of the examples of practical reasoning Aristotle gives are not of this form, but are more like syllogisms. (It is, of course, customary to call all the fragments of practical reasoning to be found in Aristotle 'practical syllogisms', but *'syllogismos'* in Greek is not as technical a term as 'syllogism' in English.) Perhaps the fullest such syllogism given by Aristotle is the following from the *De Motu Animalium* (701a18):

> I need a covering
> A cloak is a covering
> I need a cloak
> I must make what I need
> I need a cloak
> I must make a cloak

And the conclusion, 'I must make a cloak', Aristotle observes, is an action. Practical premisses, he says, come in two kinds: the good and the possible. That is, the premisses of practical reasoning set out our desires or our duties, and the possibilities which the facts of the case leave open.

I do not know how Aristotle would have formalized the syllogism I have just quoted. It looks like: 'A is B, C is A, so C is B; B is D, C is B, so C is D'. Here all the premisses are neither universal nor particular but indefinite. According to the doctrine of the *Prior Analytics* (26a29, 2927), indefinite premisses are to be treated as particulars. This would make the first half of the syllogism 'Some A is B, some C is A, some C is B.' But all syllogisms of this form are invalid. From two particular premisses no conclusion can be derived: if we are to get a conclusion we must take at least one of the premisses as universal. But the premiss 'I need all coverings' is absurd. 'All cloaks are coverings' is true; but the syllogism 'Some A is B, all C is A, some C is B' is invalid (IAI in first figure); the syllogism 'Some A is B, all A is C, some C is B' is valid (IAI in third figure); but for this we would need to read the second premiss as the falsehood 'all coverings are cloaks'. I do not see how to make Aristotle's example valid within the rules of his own syllogistic; nor is this a defect of his syllogistic, for considered as a theoretical syllogism the argument is certainly invalid, as would be the precisely parallel argument:

> I met an animal
> An elephant is an animal
> I met an elephant

The argument which I constructed from the *Metaphysics* passage is also formally invalid as a piece of theoretical reasoning, like the railway example considered earlier.

Yet, allowing for the archaic medicine, and fashion, the fragments of practical reasoning given by Aristotle do not seem at all implausible. They are appropriate verbalizations of reasons of the kind which are operative with us when we make up our minds what to do. Is there any way of making them formally valid?

Before answering this, let us consider a difficulty from a different field. Logicians have long been perturbed by forms of imperative inference which appear by the laws of assertoric logic to be unimpeachable and yet which go against our intuitions of what inferences should be possible. One well-known example is the inference from 'Post the letter' to 'post the letter or burn the letter'. Another might be the inference from 'Vote for the Labour candidate to 'Vote for somebody'. The inference from '$\phi ix\psi x$' to '$\exists x\phi x$' is perfectly valid; yet the first exhortation has hardly been obeyed by somebody who obeys the second by voting for the Conservative candidate.

Practical reasoning and imperative inference appear to be

connected. Following Hare, Stenius, and ultimately Frege, we have already distinguished in sentences between a *phrastic* (which contains the descriptive content of the sentence) and a mark of mood—assertoric or imperative—which Hare now calls a *tropic*. An imperative sentence and the corresponding assertoric sentence have the same phrastic, but a different tropic. So does the corresponding expression of intention which might conclude a piece of practical reasoning.

Earlier, we classed expressions of intention and commands together as fiats. This suggests that what we need is a logic of fiats. Plans and projects are examples of fiats. Practical reasoning, therefore, by which we work out plans, and imperative inference, in which we pass from one directive to another, can both be regarded as exemplifying a single pattern of inference which leads from fiat to fiat.

Once we extend the apparatus of formal logic to sentences in moods other than the indicative, we have to consider the relationship between the symbols of logic (in particular the logical constants and quantifiers) and the sign of mood or tropic. In particular we have to consider the order in which these symbols are to be attached to phrastics in order to make well-formed formulae of imperative logic. Consider a sentence such as 'Open the door or open the window.' Is this to be symbolized as '$\mathfrak{F}Apq$' or as '$A\mathfrak{F}p\mathfrak{F}q$'? That is to say, is a disjunctive command to be considered as the result of adding an imperative tropic to a disjunctive phrastic, or as the result of an operation by the disjunctive operator on two sentences each consisting of phrastic plus tropic? A similar question arises for conjunction, and a connected, but more complicated, one for implication.

Hare in the *Language of Morals* assumes that logical constants, when they occur in imperative or assertoric sentences, can occur only within the tropic, so that every sentence begins with a tropic and contains never more than a single tropic.[3] To me, too, this now seems the appropriate rule to adopt.

Other writers, however, think otherwise, and there was a time when I did so too. 'In "if p then q" ' I wrote the variables take the place, not of sentence-radicals [= phrastics], but of something

---

[3] 'In their ordinary uses the common logical connectives "if", "and", and "or", like the sign of negation, are best treated as part of the phrastics of sentences.' 21.

which on the face of it itself has a mood. "If the pubs are open, be sure to have a drink" is quite different from "if the pubs are open, you are sure to be having a drink" '.[4] This example does not prove what I then wanted it to prove: because of course the difference between the two sentences can be represented as a difference between $ⒺCpq$ and $ℱCpq$ as well as a difference between $CⒺpⒺp$ and $CⒺpℱq$.[5] But stronger reasons than the one I gave have been put forward for allowing tropics to occur within logical constants, and these we must now consider.

The first is drawn from the existence of conditional commands. If tropics are not allowed to occur within the scope of logical constants, then it seems that all conditional commands must be capable of translation into commands to bring about the truth of a material implication in the manner which I just suggested. But it does not seem that this is always possible. In the case of bets, there is certainly a difference between a conditional bet and a bet on the truth of a material conditional. If I bet you £5 that if p then q, then I win my money if not p; but if I say 'If p, then I bet you £5 that q', then if not p the bet is off and neither of us wins. Is there not a parallel difference in the case of commands? There is the command 'Bring it about that Cpq' which is obeyed by bringing it about that not p; and there is the conditional command 'If p, bring it about that q'—a command which, if p is not the case, is simply void. The difference, it might be said, could be well brought out by imagining the command that q to be given in sealed orders, only to be opened in the event that p.[6]

There is, I think, a genuine difference here; but it does not call for the admission of the imperative neustic within the phrastic, but rather for a further application of the distinction between fiats and directives. Directives, it will be remembered, are commands and requests: fiats which are issued for execution by the person to whom they are uttered. If we make explicit this reference to agency, then we get two different phrastics:

(1) seeing-to-it by you that if p, then q

(2) if p, seeing-to-it by you that q

[4] *Action, Emotion and Will*, 228.

[5] Here and elsewhere I use the Polish notation for the truth-functional connectives, writing 'Kpq' for 'p and q', 'Apq' for 'p or q', 'Cpq' for 'if p then q' and 'Epq' for 'p if and only if (iff) q'.

[6] Cf. M. Dummett, 'Truth', 57.

By applying the imperative tropic to these two phrastics, we get the two different commands ('D' for 'seeing-to-it-by-you').

(3) $\mathfrak{F}DCpq$
(4) $\mathfrak{F}CpDq$

These are different commands, as may be seen if we reflect that a man might be in a position to carry out the one but not the other. Suppose, for instance, he has no control over q, and has control over p which he can only exercise if commanded to do so. Then he cannot obey (4), for if p happens he is powerless to prevent q; but he can obey (3), for he can ensure the truth of Cpq by falsifying p, on the authority of the command he has been given.

But the difference between these two commands derives from the different phrastics, and not from any difference in the placing of the imperative tropics. This may be seen by noticing the difference in the assertoric between

(5) $\mathfrak{E}DCpq$
(6) $\mathfrak{E}CpDq$

It is sufficient to make the second, but not the first, of these is true if not p should occur through no fault of yours.

Professor Castaneda[7] has put forward two arguments against the thesis that logical constants belong within phrastics. We can distinguish from each other the apparently imperative sentences

(a) You, Paul, are going to shut the door, or you, Abel, shut it.
(b) You, Abel, are going to shut the door, or you, Paul, shut it.
(c) You, Abel, or you, Paul, shut the door.

The differences, says Castaneda, are quite clear.

(a) tells Abel that he is to shut the door if Paul does not; (b) does not tell Abel to shut the door at all. Moreover, (b) tells Paul to shut the door, while (a) does nothing of the kind. (c) does not tell either Paul or Abel individually to shut the door. Yet on Hare's view, either (a) or (b) are both meaningless, or both are indistinguishable from each other as well as from (c). Both (a) and (b) are meaningless if they are regarded as made up of two sentences linked by the logical word 'or'. All three are indistinguishable from one another if they are regarded as being made up of the neustic 'please' attached to a complex

[7] See his paper 'Imperatives, Decisions and "Oughts"'.

of two phrastics connected by the logical word 'or', namely '(You, Paul, going to shut the door, or you, Abel, going to shut the door) please.'

The three sentences quoted by Castaneda are certainly distinct; and they are all meaningful; but they do not provide an argument against the thesis of the *Language of Morals*. This is because they violate rules which are tacitly applied whenever real-life sentences are produced as instances of logical formulae. For instance, if 'Queen Anne is dead or Queen Anne is not dead' is given as an instance of $ApNp$ it is taken for granted that the Queen Anne intended is the same in each case and not, e.g., Anne of Austria in the first sentence and Anne of Cleves in the second. Castaneda's examples, in allowing 'you' to mean 'Paul' in one case and 'Abel' in the other, violate this rule. It might be objected that this is covered by the addition of 'Paul' and 'Abel' in apposition: just as 'Queen Anne of Austria is dead or Queen Anne of Cleves is not dead' is perfectly well formed, though not an instance of $ApNp$. But this reply too is inadequate. For 'you' is a token-reflexive: it is equivalent to: 'the person to whom this sentence is uttered' and so it must already be settled what counts as *this sentence* before the person indicated by 'you' can be ascertained. Castaneda's alleged sentences consist of two parts, one part uttered to Abel and the other uttered to Paul; consequently, 'you' can indicate a different person in each part. But if we allow such sentences as substitution instances of formulae of propositional calculus, then even in the assertoric mood we run into absurdity. 'You are wearing a grey suit and you are not wearing a grey suit' is true if I address first you, and then you; Castaneda could as well urge it as a counter-instance to the principle of contradiction as urge the instances he gives against Hare.

Castaneda has another argument, which I shall discuss in terms of an example other than the one he gives (228). Suppose that I say 'Long live the King of France.' How are we to apply to this Russell's theory of descriptions? The phrastic will presumably be

For some x, x's being King of France, and for all y, y's being King of France only if $y = x$, and x's living long.

But what tropic shall we attach? If we attach 𝕰, then it is a statement that the King of France lives long; if we attach 𝕱, then it becomes the wish that there *were* some x which etc. Perhaps it might be said it does not matter; the Russellian analysis here merely makes explicit a wish implicit in the unanalysed wish, just as the Russellian analysis of assertions makes explicit assertions which are presupposed in the unanalysed assertion. In this case, this does not seem too unplausible. But 'To hell with the Pope' is not plausibly represented as containing implicitly a desire that anybody should be Pope at all.

To some defenders of Hare's account—already disposed on other grounds to question Russell's theory—this seems one further argument in favour of an alternative position. To others, it does seem a serious argument in favour of placing an imperative tropic after the first two clauses and before the third: i.e. for having tropics within phrastics. In my view, it provides a reason for believing—as I shall later argue—that the rules of inference in practical reasoning differ from those in theoretical.

The main positive reason for keeping tropics out of phrastics is the enormous gain in simplicity. If the logical constants can occur outside tropics, they need wholly redefining. They are defined by their truth-values, but if they are to conjoin not only statements but commands then definition will no longer be adequate. Moreover, if tropics are kept outside phrastics, there is no need to have special formation rules for tropics; the rule is simply that tropics may be added to any well-formed phrastic. On the other hand, if we allow the logical constants to construct molecular sentences out of atomic sentences in different moods, then we shall have to work out rules for the moods of the resulting sentences given the moods of the component sentences, just as we have rules for working out the truth-values of complex sentences for possible combinations of truth-values for their simple components. In some cases this does not seem difficult. A conditional whose antecedent and consequent are both assertoric is clearly itself assertoric; so we will have $C\mathfrak{C}\mathfrak{C} = \mathfrak{C}$. A conditional whose antecedent is assertoric and whose consequent is imperative seems to be a command; so we have $C\mathfrak{C}\mathfrak{F} = \mathfrak{F}$; but what are we to say of $C\mathfrak{F}\mathfrak{C}$? It is hard to think of anything which would be an instance of this. 'If you are going to be such a wet blanket, go home' ($C\mathfrak{C}\mathfrak{F}$) is all right; but 'If go home, you are going to be such a wet blanket' seems ill formed. So too with sentences of the form '$C\mathfrak{F}\mathfrak{C}$'. 'If go away come back soon' is ill formed; it sounds, in fact, like pidgin for 'If you go away come back soon' which is $C\mathfrak{C}\mathfrak{F}$.

If simplicity were all that were in question, it might be argued that this did not matter. Truth-tables, it is often said, supply truth-values to complex sentences where ordinary language does not (e.g. conditionals with false antecedents). Similarly, here logic will supply moods to sentences which in ordinary language do not have moods, and declare well-formed sentences which in ordinary language sound bizarre. So long as the rules coincide with ordinary language in the cases where ordinary language has rules, this will not matter.

But this is not enough. The effect of the suggested rules for operating with tropics is such as to wreck even the simplest laws governing the use of the logical constants. For instance, contraposition. The rule that from Cpq we can infer $CNqNp$ holds for the assertoric mood and for the imperative mood. But what of the alleged mixed moods? $C\mathfrak{C}p\mathfrak{F}q$ is perfectly all right; and it is apparently an imperative. But $CN\mathfrak{F}q\mathfrak{C}p$ is not an imperative; it is simply ill formed.

Again, Cpq is by definition, in many systems, and by tautology in all systems, equivalent to $ANpq$. But whereas if $\mathfrak{F}p$ and $\mathfrak{F}q$ are well-formed imperatives, $A\mathfrak{F}p\mathfrak{F}q$ sounds well enough, it is not the case that where $AN\mathfrak{F}p\mathfrak{F}q$ is well formed, $C\mathfrak{F}p\mathfrak{F}q$ is well formed. And what are we to say of sentences formed by the conjunction of assertions and imperatives? Is $K\mathfrak{F}p\mathfrak{F}q$ an assertion or an imperative? If an assertion, what are its truth conditions? If an imperative, what are its satisfaction conditions?

From all this we can see that the thesis of the *Language of Morals* is the best solution to the problem of the formation rules for the logic of practical inference. What, then, of the transformation rules? These must surely depend on the value to be presumed in practical reasoning: on the practical analogue of truth.

Practical reasoning, I have said, can very well be looked at as a process of passing from one fiat to another according to rules, just as theoretical reasoning consists in passing from one assertoric sentence to another according to rules. The point of the rules for theoretical reasoning is to ensure that one never passes from true assertions to false assertions. What then is the practical analogue?

Fiats contain descriptions of possible states of affairs whose actualization satisfies the desires expressed by them. Among fiats, we have noted, are plans and projects. We can distinguish, among plans and projects, between those which are executed and those which are not executed. But when we are discussing the merits of plans, one thing we are looking for is a plan which will be *satisfactory*. Now of course a plan may be unsatisfactory precisely because it will be difficult to execute: but being executed and being satisfactory are in fact two quite different things. Commonly, in discussing plans, we presuppose our ability to implement them, and try to work out which, of the various plans we might implement, is most satisfactory—i.e. which will best serve our purposes and gratify our desires. We might be inclined to say: what is satisfactory is not the plan, but the state of affairs projected by the plan. Certainly, it is true that a state of affairs may be satisfactory or unsatisfactory; but it would be absurd to say that a plan was not satisfactory simply on the grounds that it was only a plan and not yet executed. For much of practical reasoning consists in the search for a satisfactory plan to execute; if a plan were never satisfactory unless executed, planning would be impossible. For we would have to do everything in our power before we could decide which of the things in our power was the best thing to do; and by then it would be too late.

Obviously satisfactoriness is a relative notion. Execution and non-execution, like truth and falsehood, are absolute notions; an assertion is either true or false, a command is either executed or not. But a plan is not just either satisfactory or not satisfactory: it may be satisfactory to some persons and not to others, satisfactory for some purposes and not for others.

Let us suppose that we desire a certain state of affairs for its own sake, and not as a means to any further end. Then the fiat which expresses this desire will, obviously, be a fiat whose satisfaction will satisfy the desire. Let us call such a *goal-fiat*, and say that it expresses a *purpose*. We are free to settle our purposes; but it does not depend on us which plans are compatible with, or effective of, the achievement of our purposes. Independently of us, certain states of affairs and certain plans are unsatisfactory to certain purposes; viz. those which are incompatible with the desired state of affairs. Independently also of us, any plan whose realization involves the actualization of the desired state of affairs will be satisfactory *for that purpose*. We cannot guarantee that it will be satisfactory to us (for it may conflict with other purposes of ours) still less that it will be satisfactory to all other persons.

Reflection on these considerations led me to suggest, some years ago,[8] that the logic operative in practical reasoning was the logic of *satisfactoriness*. This was to consist of the rules which ensure that in practical reasoning we never pass from a fiat which is satisfactory for a particular purpose to a fiat which is unsatisfactory for that purpose. These rules are satisfactoriness-preserving just as rules for assertoric inference are truth-preserving. Trivially, every fiat is satisfactory relative to the purpose expressed by itself.

It is not difficult to construct such a logic of satisfactoriness. First, we must distinguish between *satisfactoriness* and *satisfaction*. A fiat $\mathfrak{F}p$ is satisfied just in case the corresponding assertion $\mathfrak{E}p$ is true. Clearly, a logic of satisfaction would be an exact and uninteresting parallel of assertoric logic: whenever we can infer $\mathfrak{E}q$ from $\mathfrak{E}p$ we can infer the satisfaction of $\mathfrak{F}q$ from the satisfaction of $\mathfrak{F}p$. The relation of the logic of satisfactoriness to the logic of satisfaction is this.[9] Let A and B both be fiats. B may be inferred from A in the logic of satisfaction iff necessarily whenever A is satisfied then B is satisfied. B may be inferred from A in the logic of satisfactoriness iff necessarily when A is satisfactory to a certain set of wants then B is satisfactory to that set of wants. Rules of inference in the logic of satisfaction are satisfaction-preserving: i.e. they are designed to prevent one passing from a satisfied fiat to an unsatisfied fiat. (They are in fact precisely analogous to the truth-preserving rules of assertoric inference which are designed to prevent one passing from a true premiss to a false conclusion.) Rules of inference in the logic of satisfactoriness are satisfactoriness-preserving: i.e. they are designed to prevent one passing from a satisfactory fiat (plan) to an unsatisfactory fiat. Now a plan is satisfactory relative to a certain set of wants, if and only if whenever the plan is satisfied every member of that set of wishes is satisfied. If it can be proved that if A is satisfied B is satisfied, then it follows that if B is satisfactory A is satisfactory. Again, if it is the

---

[8] In an article 'Practical Inference' (*Analysis*, 1966) on which part of this chapter is based.

[9] In what follows the 'propositional variables' p, q, r are to be taken to range over unasserted phrastics; P, Q, R, are metalogical variables to represent expressions built up out of p, q, r, etc., and logical constants; A, B, are metalogical variables to represent expressions built up from the type of expression represented by P, Q, R, plus either an assertoric or imperative tropic.

case that if A is satisfactory B is satisfactory, then it follows that if B is satisfied A is satisfied. 'Satisfactory' in the last two sentences, of course, means 'satisfactory relative to a given set of wishes or goals'. It follows from all this that the logic of satisfactoriness is the mirror image of the logic of satisfaction. That is to say, whenever the logic of satisfaction permits the inference from A to B, the logic of satisfactoriness permits the inference from B to A.

It is impossible to base the logic of satisfactoriness on satisfactoriness-tables, because satisfactoriness, unlike truth, is a relative notion. But because of the mirror-image relationship between the logics of satisfaction and satisfactoriness it is possible to test the validity of inferences in the logic of satisfactoriness by appeal to truth-tables and quantificational truths. Suppose that we wish to know whether $\mathfrak{F}$P can be derived from $\mathfrak{F}$Q in the propositional calculus of satisfactoriness: i.e. whether, if $\mathfrak{F}$Q is satisfactory, $\mathfrak{F}$P is satisfactory also. The answer is that the inference is valid if CPQ is tautologous. For instance, you wish to know whether $\mathfrak{F}Kpq$ can be inferred from $\mathfrak{F}Apq$. To test whether it can, you write $CKpq\ Apq$ and test for tautology in the usual manner.

The reason for this is obvious. If CPQ is tautologous, then if $\mathfrak{E}$P is true, $\mathfrak{E}$Q is true; so if $\mathfrak{F}$P is satisfied, $\mathfrak{F}$Q is satisfied; so if $\mathfrak{F}$Q is satisfactory, $\mathfrak{F}$P is satisfactory. (For if $\mathfrak{F}$Q is satisfactory, then if $\mathfrak{F}$Q is satisfied all the members of G are satisfied; if $\mathfrak{F}$P is satisfied, $\mathfrak{F}$Q is satisfied; so if $\mathfrak{F}$P is satisfied, all the members of G are satisfied; so $\mathfrak{F}$P is satisfactory.) So to with the predicate calculus of satisfactoriness: if CPQ is a quantificational truth, then $\mathfrak{F}$P can be inferred from $\mathfrak{F}$Q. In general: if CQP is a logical law, then $\mathfrak{F}$P yields $\mathfrak{F}$Q in the logic of satisfactoriness.

The logic of satisfactoriness offers a means of solving some of the puzzles which disturbed us. The inference from 'Post the letter' to 'Post the letter or burn the letter' is not valid in this logic, and this conforms with our intuitive expectations. So too, the inference from 'Vote for the Labour candidate' to 'Vote for someone' is invalid. On the other hand, the inference from 'Post the letter or burn the letter' to 'Burn the letter', which is invalid in the logic of satisfaction, is valid in this logic; and the validity of this is recognized by anyone who realizes that he can obey the order 'post the letter or burn the letter' by burning the letter. So too, the logic of satisfactoriness contains an explicit law justifying the inference from 'Vote for someone' to 'Vote for the Labour candidate' which would be tacitly adopted by anyone who obeyed the first order by voting Labour.

The logic of satisfactoriness has certain features which *prima facie* appear paradoxical. For instance, in this logic the inference 'Kill the conspirators; Brutus is a conspirator; so kill Brutus' is invalid. But this result, properly understood, is perfectly correct: the order 'Kill the conspirators' has not been fully obeyed by someone who obeys the order 'Kill Brutus' unless Brutus is the only conspirator, which the premisses do not entitle us to conclude. Again, in the logic of satisfactoriness there is an inference from $\mathfrak{F}p$ to $\mathfrak{F}Kpq$, since assertorically $\mathfrak{F}Kpq$ entails $\mathfrak{F}p$. But surely one cannot infer 'open the door and smash the window' from 'open the door'! In answer, we may agree first that the *command* 'open the door and smash the window' can't be inferred from the *command* 'open the door': the logic of satisfactoriness concerns fiats, not directives. From the command 'open the door' one can, however, infer the fiat '$\mathfrak{F}$ (opening of the door and smashing of the window)'; someone who did execute such a plan would indeed obey the original command and satisfy the desire which that command might vent. By executing the command in such a manner, the agent would no doubt annoy the commander; but this would be because he would be acting against the commander's tacit desire that the window should not be broken. If this tacit desire were made explicit, the fiat expressing the commander's state of mind would be of the form $\mathfrak{F}KpNq$; from which there is no inference in the logic of satisfactoriness to $\mathfrak{F}Kpq$. Thus the paradox here is only apparent.

In the logic of satisfactoriness, we can pass from $\mathfrak{F}q$ to $\mathfrak{F}KpCpq$. In other words, the analogue of affirming the consequent is not a fallacy in the logic of satisfactoriness. This gives us a clue how to deal with Aristotle's example, 'He is to be heated; if I rub him he will be heated; so I'll rub him', which was invalid in his own logic. Similarly, the inference from $\mathfrak{F}\exists x\phi x$ to $\mathfrak{F}\phi a$ is valid in the logic of satisfactoriness; and this suggests a way to deal with the cloak syllogism.[10]

---

[10] Aristotle's cloak syllogism in fact contains mixed premisses, one imperative setting out a goal, and one assertoric setting out the facts of the case. A possible rule for such inferences is this. Remove the assertoric tropics from the assertoric premisses: conjoin their phrastics with the phrastics of the imperative conclusions and assign an imperative tropic

But though the logic of satisfactoriness provides a solution for a number of familiar paradoxes, many people have been repelled by the paradoxes which it is thought to generate in its turn. In fact the application of the logic of satisfactoriness leads to no genuinely paradoxical conclusions, and it is undoubtedly sound in the sense that the application of its rules will preserve from premiss to conclusion the designated value of satisfactoriness. The alleged paradoxical inferences are all instances of overkill, whether metaphorical or literal. But if we object to the line of reasoning 'The newborn claimant to the Kingship of Israel is to be killed; the newborn claimant to the Kingship of Israel is an infant in Bethlehem; so all the infants in Bethlehem are to be killed' it is not Herod's *logic* that we are faulting.[11]

This much, however, must be conceded to the critics of the

---

to this conjunction. Then the inference is valid in imperative logic if an assertion corresponding to the goal-fiat can be derived in assertoric logic from the conjunction of the other premisses and the conclusion (e.g.' $\mathfrak{F}p$ $\mathfrak{F}Cqp$; so $\mathfrak{F}q$' is valid in practical reasoning because '$KCqpq$' entails 'p'). The rationale of this is twofold. (1) In order to begin practical reasoning one must accept the facts as they are (e.g. one cannot reason practically about Communist China without accepting its existence) and this corresponds to replacing the assertion with the corresponding fiat. (2) The means chosen must be sufficient for the goal to be reached; and this will be so when the conclusion conjoined with the other premisses entails, in theoretical logic, the goal-premiss's assertoric equivalent. But the complications introduced by mixed premisses make it difficult to formalize Aristotle's examples just as they stand.

[11] Thus Alf Ross' criticism of the logic of satisfactoriness (*Directives and Norms*, 176) misses the point. Professor Anscombe, who agrees in rejecting Ross' complaint ('Von Wright on Practical Inference, . . .'), says that the inference from $\mathfrak{F}p$ to $\mathfrak{F}(Kpq)$ is acceptable only when effecting two things is *a way* of effecting one of them, so that the second fiat would be a description of a single action: it would be futile, having effected that p, to go on later to effect that q in satisfaction of the original wish that p. Her point shows that the logic of satisfactoriness concerns merely the relations between states of affairs qua want-satisfactions: in order to be applied to the *bringing about* of states of affairs—and thus to become a genuinely practical logic, rather than a wish-fulfilment logic ensnaring Midases and useful only to fairy godmothers—it needs supplementing with a logic of the description of actions. Von Wright in a number of papers (most recently 'Handlungslogik' in *Normenlogik*, ed. Lenk) has outlined such a logic: in a form, however, which enshrines the implausible axiom that one brings it about that p and q if and only if one brings it about that p and one brings it about that q.

logic of satisfactoriness, that it is misleading to call it 'the logic of practical reasoning'. I once argued its claim to that name in the following way:

> The logic of satisfactoriness, and not the logic of satisfaction, is the principal logic of imperatives. This is because the purpose of practical reasoning is to get done what we want; just as the purpose of theoretical reasoning is to discover truth. The preservation of satisfactoriness, therefore, has in practical inference that place which the preservation of truth has in theoretical inference. Those rules will most deserve the name 'rules of practical inference' which will ensure that in reasoning about what to do we never pass from a plan which will satisfy our desires to a plan which will not satisfy them. And these rules are the rules of the logic of satisfactoriness. (art. cit. p. 73)

There are, I now think, two things which are misleading about this. The first is that in speaking of a 'logic of imperatives' and of a 'logic of practical reasoning' one may be thought to be suggesting that in issuing imperatives and in reasoning out our plans we are making use of a set of logical truths different from those which are formalized in the familiar propositional and predicate calculus and the modal systems built on them. And this is certainly not so: one and the same set of logical truths is exploited in both assertoric and practical reasoning. And so if logics are individuated by the set of logical truths which they formalize, there is not a logic of commands which differs from the logic of statements, nor a logic of practical reasoning which differs from the logic of theoretical reasoning.

However, it is possible to think of logic as primarily the study of patterns of inference rather than the formalization of logical truths. Historically, both approaches have been made dominant in the work of different authors. The traditional 'Aristotelian' logic concentrates almost exclusively on valid patterns of inference, and has little to say about logical truths. Wittgenstein's *Tractatus*, by attempting to reduce all propositions to truth-functions of logically unrelated elementary propositions, and by offering truth-tables to display the relationships between different truth-functions, made the notion of logical truth dominant and attempted to render rules of inference superfluous. Most contemporary logical systems employ both logical truths and rules of inference: in axiomatic systems such as Frege's the logical truths which are the axioms and theorems are dominant, and rules of inference within the system are applied only to logical truths; in natural deduction systems such as Gentzen's it is the rules of inference which are basic; they are applied to non-logical propositions and the logical truths are yielded only as the results of particular applications of the rules.

In assertoric logic, to every valid inference schema there corresponds a logically true conditional statement, and to every logically true conditional statement there corresponds a valid inference schema; so that it may seem to be a matter merely of combinatorial elegance, not of philosophical importance which approach is taken. But of course when we turn to study the logic of imperatives or fiats, the matter is quite different. For here, it seems, we can take only the rules-of-inference approach. For commands, requests, and wishes, not having truth-values at all, *a fortiori* cannot be logical truths.

But even in the assertoric case there is an ambiguity in speaking of 'logical truth'. A logically true assertion is not the same thing as a logically true proposition. 'Truth' as applied to propositions must be distinguished from 'Truth' as applied to assertions. This point was brought out very clearly by Erik Stenius in his book *Wittgenstein's Tractatus*. Stenius distinguishes between *descriptive* truth and *modal* truth. Descriptive truth and descriptive falsehood are properties of phrastics or sentence-radicals: a phrastic has descriptive truth if there is in reality a state of affairs answering to it. Modal truth is a property only of sentences in a particular *mood*, namely the assertoric. If—with a degree of oversimplification, as Stenius admits—we take the indicative mood as the mood of assertion, then an assertion is a move in a language-game whose principle is:

(A) Produce a sentence in the indicative mood only if the sentence-radical is a true description.

The word 'true' in this rule refers to the concept of truth as applied to sentence-radicals; the concept of 'truth' as applied to assertions is a different one and can thus be defined in terms of it without circularity. Stenius observes:

The concept of truth appearing in the moral rule 'Always

speak the truth' is the modal truth. The moral rule says that you must always play the language-game of the indicative mood correctly, not that you must always produce true sentence-radicals. Only the existence of rule (A) makes it possible to deceive people by breaking it.

It is not difficult to produce the corresponding rule for the imperative:

(B) Produce a sentence in the imperative mood only if the sentence-radical is to be made true.[12]

The notion of descriptive truth thus enters into an account of the imperative as well as of the indicative mood. But clearly descriptive truth is separable both from assertoric truth and from the correct use of imperatives. An assertion of a conditional, If p then q, may be a true assertion even though both the phrastics, p and q are false—descriptively false, that is, for being unasserted they have no assertoric truth-value, are neither true nor false assertions. The felicitous utterance of an imperative on the other hand, actually presupposes that the sentence-radical it involves is descriptively false; for only if it is false can it be made true. And clearly the notion of assertoric truth applies neither to the phrastic of the command nor to the command as a whole.

Now when we speak of logical truth what we are principally concerned with is descriptive or propositional truth, not assertoric truth. Of course, someone who asserts a proposition which is a logical truth—a description which is true in virtue of its logical form—will *eo ipso* make a logically true assertion. But the truth which logic is ultimately concerned with is the descriptive truth of propositions which are themselves neutral with regard to the various speech-acts which may employ them as phrastics or sentence-radicals. In this sense there are not two logics, one assertoric and one imperative: there is one logic, which is itself neither assertoric nor imperative, but propositional and which is used in different ways in commands and statements, in practical and in theoretical reasoning.

[12] Stenius' own rule is 'Make the sentence radical true'—obviously a rule directed to the listener, not the speaker. This seems to be an incorrect formulation of the rule; it would have the consequence that disobedience to a command was always an abuse of language, parallel to a lie.

We can thus see what is correct and what is incorrect in talking about 'the logic of practical reasoning'. The other thing which was misleading in my earlier remarks about the logic of satisfactoriness is this. I said that the purpose of practical reasoning was to get done what we want, while the purpose of theoretical reasoning is to discover truth. This, I think, is correct, but it does not follow from that by itself that the logic of satisfactoriness is the practical analogue of theoretical formal logic. Because in getting done what we want we have to make use of the logic of satisfaction as well as the logic of satisfactoriness; and in the discovery of truth we make use not only of deductive logic but of 'inductive logic' as well. So that what we have to examine is not simply the relationship between two terms, theoretical and practical logic, but between four terms, theoretical deductive and theoretical inductive logic, and the practical logic of satisfaction and satisfactoriness.

This was very clearly brought out in Professor Hare's paper, 'Practical Inferences' (pp. 59–73 of his book of that name). When we have to fulfil commands and intentions, Hare explained, we have to reason from them to the necessary and sufficient conditions for fulfilling them. The Aristotelian examples of practical reasonings, he says, are some of them reasonings to necessary conditions (as in 'Everyone is to march, so I'm to march'), and some of them reasonings to sufficient conditions (as in: I must have a covering, so I must have a cloak), and Aristotle did not pay sufficient attention to the difference between these two. The logic of satisfaction and the logic of satisfactoriness, Hare maintains, correspond respectively to reasoning to necessary conditions and reasoning to sufficient conditions. These do not amount to a new 'imperative logic'; for reasoning to sufficient conditions no less than reasoning to necessary conditions occurs in the assertoric as well as the imperative case.

The logic of necessary and sufficient conditions is a well-worn application of ordinary logic; and so it is not necessary to claim that Kenny's logic of satisfactoriness, when redescribed as a logic of sufficient conditions, introduces any element peculiar to imperatives or practical inferences. It might be the case (though, as we shall see, it is not) that in practical reasoning we always inferred sufficient conditions, and in theoretical reasoning never. In actual fact, the most that can be said is that reasoning to sufficient conditions is somewhat commoner (because more commonly useful) in practical thought than in theoretical. (loc. cit., p. 68)

We reason to necessary conditions in practical contexts, for example, when we are seeking to obey a negative prohibition; and we reason to sufficient conditions in theoretical contexts, for instance, when we are seeking an explanation, whether in scientific contexts of theory building or in ordinary life as when we reason thus: 'Harry is late; but the 10.45 being late is something that would make Harry late; so (perhaps) the 10.45 is late.' Inferences to explanation, Hare shows, are isomorphic to inferences in the logic of satisfactoriness.

The considerations which Hare adduces show that the mirror-image relationship between theoretical and practical reasoning is more complicated than at first appears. In theoretical argument it is reasoning to necessary conditions—deductive theoretical logic —which is *conclusive*, in the sense of ensuring that the conclusion has the value which the reasoning aims at, namely truth; only deductive inference makes it certain that if the premises are true the conclusion is also. Inference to the best explanation, or inductive logic, as a host of philosophers of science have insisted, is never conclusive in the sense of showing that it is logically impossible for the premises to be true and the conclusion false. On the other hand, in practical inference it is only the logic of satisfactoriness which is *conclusive*, in the sense of ensuring that the conclusion has the value that the reasoning aims at, namely the satisfaction of the reasoner's wants. The logic of satisfaction— reasoning to necessary conditions for satisfaction—is never conclusive in the sense of ensuring the arrival of what is wanted. Having carried out a piece of practical reasoning to necessary conditions, and put the conclusion into action, the reasoner cannot then rest secure in the confidence that what he has done will bring about the state of affairs he wants: there may be *more* that he has to do in order to achieve his goals. In particular, to take Hare's example, one never comes to the end of satisfying a negative prohibition. In real life, both practical and theoretical inference is a mixture of both kinds of reasoning;[13] but

[13] I used to think that the logic of satisfactoriness alone was sufficient

the relationship of the elements so mixed differs in the two cases.

The upshot of Hare's discussion of reasoning to sufficient and necessary conditions is that the thesis of the mirror-image relationship between theoretical and practical reasoning needs complication rather than recantation. He offers also, however, a more searching criticism of the theory based on the notions of assent and consistency.

> According to the logic of satisfactoriness, I can deduce the command 'Shut the door' from the command 'Shut the door or shut the window'. But in the case of ordinary valid logical inferences he who assents to the premisses is *compelled* not to dissent from the conclusion, on pain of logical inconsistency. It might be suggested that with the present inference this rule does not hold. I can without any inconsistency agree to shut the door or shut the window, and then refuse to shut the door provided that I shut the window.

It can, as Hare agrees, be replied to this that to assent, in the logic of satisfactoriness, is to find what is assented to satisfactory for a given purpose. But this reply seems to strain the meaning of 'assent': to assent to a command—to say 'Yes' to something like 'Shut the door'—is surely to agree to obey it; to assent to a plan— to say 'Yes' to something like 'Let's have a picnic'—is to agree to execute it. And surely someone may without any inconsistency assent to a fiat in that sense without assenting to another fiat which is derivable from it in the logic of satisfactoriness: to use another of Hare's examples one may assent to 'Book me a room in the best hotel in town' and fail to assent to 'Book me all the rooms in all the hotels in town'.

Consideration of this example brings out a point which we encountered earlier, that the logic of commands is more complicated than the logic of fiats in general. In particular, if we are to discuss the notion of assent to a command, we have to give different accounts of commander's assent (e.g. what commands he would

for practical reasoning and that cases of 'reasoning to necessary conditions' could be dealt with as cases of reasoning, in the logic of satisfactoriness, to conditions which were both sufficient and necessary. But, as Professor Anscombe has pointed out to me, this won't deal with such inferences as 'I'll never get to the station tomorrow unless I pack this case tonight; so I will pack it tonight'.

regard as validly drawn transmissions of his commands down a chain of command) and commandee's assent (e.g. what other commands he is committed to accepting in virtue of having accepted a given command). This is a difficult topic which it is fortunately not necessary to pursue in attempting to give an account of practical reasoning: the difficulty which Hare points out suffices to show that the logic of satisfactoriness needs very drastic supplementation if it is to be regarded as the logic of commands.

However, Hare's objection does not seem to me to be equally damaging to the proposal to assign a central place to the logic of satisfactoriness in the case of practical reasoning, and reasoning about fiats in general. For if someone has expressed his current wants adequately in a goal-fiat, then there *is* something inconsistent in his refusing to welcome a fiat which is derivable from it in the logic of satisfactoriness. If my *only* want is to have the door open, why should I object if someone opens the door and smashes the window? Of course, there is something insane in the idea of having only a single want of that kind; and the reason I would object in the case in point is that I don't want the window smashed. But if that is among my wants, then it should be included in the goal-fiat from which the practical reasoning starts. If I dislike a conclusion to which a piece of practical reasoning leads, then it shows that I have inadequately specified my goals; and if I am to be consistent I must revise my goals, review the list of purposes which constitute my goal-fiat.

This feature of practical reasoning has led some people to the belief that the logic of satisfactoriness is really only an enthymematic version of the logic of satisfaction: a piece of practical reasoning in the logic of satisfactoriness is really a piece of reasoning in the logic of satisfaction with some of its premisses suppressed. Consider the example given earlier

I am to be in London at 4.15
If I catch the 2.30 I'll be in London at 4.15
So I'll catch the 2.30.

This is valid, it is suggested, only because it is enthymematic, with an unstated premiss reflecting the fact that I don't want to be in London any earlier than I have to be. If such a premiss is made explicit, then there will be a reasoning to necessary conditions, which will bring out that if I'm to be in London as close to 4.15 as possible but no later, I must take the 2.30.[14]

What such examples show is not that reasoning in the logic of satisfactoriness is enthymematic, but that it is defeasible. The reasoning is not enthymematic, for no extra premises needed to be added to ensure that the use of reasoning will lead from satisfactory premises only to a satisfactory conclusion. But the reasoning is defeasible because if we add further satisfactory premises we cannot be sure that the conclusion will remain satisfactory. Theoretical deductive reasoning is not defeasible in the sense that the addition of a premiss cannot invalidate a previously valid inference: if a conclusion follows from a given set of premises it can be drawn from any larger set containing those premises no matter how many are added to the set. With practical reasoning in the logic of satisfactoriness this is not so. Though catching the 2.30 may be a reasonable conclusion from the premises first set out, it ceases to be reasonable if we add the premises that the 2.30 is always crowded to bursting point, and that it would be a good thing to work on the train.

The defeasibility of practical reasoning has been emphasized by Geach.

> Some years ago I read a letter in a political weekly to some such effect as this. 'I do not dispute Col. Bogey's premises, nor the logic of his inference. But even if a conclusion is validly drawn from acceptable premises, we are not obliged to accept if it those premises are incomplete; and unfortunately there is a vital premise missing from the Colonel's argument—the existence of Communist China.' I do not know what Col. Bogey's original argument had been; whether this criticism of it could be apt depends on whether it was a piece of indicative or of practical reasoning. Indicative reasoning from a set of premises,

---

[14] I owe this suggestion to Professor F. Stoutland. He argues that unless the example given is enthymematic, we would have to admit the validity of the parallel reasoning.

> If I am to be in London six months hence
> If I catch today's 2.30 I'll be in London six months hence
> So I'll catch today's 2.30.

But of course, for the reasons given, there is nothing paradoxical in accepting this reasoning as valid.

if valid, could of course not be invalidated because there is a premise 'missing' from the set. But a piece of practical reasoning from a set of premises can be invalidated thus: your opponent produces a fiat you have to accept, and the addition of this to the fiats you have already accepted yields a combination with which your conclusion is inconsistent. (*Logic Matters*, 286)

Here again we can note the parallel between the practical logic of satisfactoriness and the theoretical logic of explanation. A theory that may be perfectly adequate to explain a given set of data—e.g. the Ptolemaic hypothesis—may cease to be adequate when we add new data.

The defeasibility of practical reasoning comes about because of satisfactoriness being—like explanation—a relative notion: something is not satisfactory *simpliciter*, but satisfactory relative to a given set of wants; just as something is not an explanation *simpliciter*, but an explanation of a given set of data. The only way to avoid defeasibility in practical reasoning would be to insist that the premiss setting out the goal should be not only correct but also complete; that *all* the wants to be satisfied by one's action should be fully specified. If we could do this, then there would be no danger of some further premiss being added—some further want turning up—which would negative the satisfactoriness of the action described in the solution.

Both Aristotle and St. Thomas sometimes write as if they thought that the first premiss of a piece of practical reasoning must be a universal plan of life of this kind, specifying an all-embracing good. Indeed, the type of premiss they had in mind was something not only universal, but also objective. They regarded the value to be transmitted by practical reasoning as not being satisfactoriness, but rather goodness: and goodness, in their view, was not something relative to the wants of a given individual, but something objectively discernible. For them, rules of practical reasoning would be rules designed to ensure that if the state of affairs described in the premiss which sets out the goal of the practical reasoning is good, and if the form of reasoning is valid, then the state of affairs described in the conclusion is good. Goodness in practical reasoning would then be the analogue of truth in theoretical reasoning. Moreover, just as there were self-evident truths which played a special part in the use of theoretical reason, there were, on the Aristotelian view, self-desirable goods which had the cardinal role in practical reasoning.

Such a line of thought is very alien to contemporary philosophical fashion. To attempt a serious evaluation of it would call for an extended treatise. But whether or not the objectivity of the designated value refutes the Aristotelian theory of practical reasoning, the universality of the postulated major premisses seems to me to establish the theory's inadequacy.

The notion of a premiss which is complete enough to prevent defeasibility while specific enough to entail a practical conclusion is surely chimerical. Only in restricted contexts can we even approach completeness in the specification of practical premisses: we insist, for instance, that the listing of contra-indications on a marketed drug should be not only accurate but, within limits, complete. But even if we could specify a whole plan of life in the Aristotelian manner this would only prevent defeasibility in the logic of satisfactoriness, it would not prevent the defeasibility of any Aristotelian 'logic of goodness'. It would not prevent a situation in which an action which one argument may show to be a good action may be shown by a further argument to be a bad action. This is something which Aquinas himself often insisted upon. He took this as showing, however, not that practical reasoning was defeasible, in the sense that an argument from certain premisses to the goodness of a state of affairs represented in a conclusion might by means of the addition of further premisses be rendered invalid or brought to cease to hold, but rather as showing a difference between goodness and truth. It is a presupposition of truth-functional logic that any proposition which has the value 'true' does not also have the value 'false'; but it is not the case that a proposal for action which has the value 'good' may not also have the value 'bad'. On the Thomist view an argument which shows to be bad a conclusion which another argument showed to be good need not in any way contradict that argument: it merely establishes that the proposal contained in the conclusion has both good and bad aspects. Moreover, an argument which shows something to be a good thing to do in no way shows that something incompatible with the conclusion it reaches may not also be a good thing to do.

This feature of practical reasoning was repeatedly stressed by Aquinas. It provided, he believed, the sense in which practical reasoning does not necessitate its conclusions; and he saw the contingency of the conclusions of practical reason as being the fundamental ground of the freedom of the human will.

The contrast just mentioned between truth and goodness seems to me to show that if there could be a logic of objective goodness as envisaged in the Thomist tradition it would bear no simple relation to the assertoric logic of truth. It would need, for instance, to be a three-valued system in order to allow for the possibility of actions being a mixture of good and evil without falling into plain inconsistency. I shall not hazard any conjecture about the form it might take.

The logic of satisfactoriness, however, does not present the special difficulties such a project raises: and provided that it is allowed to remain defeasible it seems neither chimerical nor unfamiliar. In the logic of satisfactoriness the analogy of the Thomist contingency of goodness is precisely the feature of defeasibility. In the following chapter, therefore, I shall try to adapt to contemporary concerns, and to my own account of practical reasoning in terms of satisfactoriness, St. Thomas' insight that the freedom of the will is bound up with the special nature of practical reasoning.

The logic of satisfactoriness is no more than a part of practical reasoning. We have already observed that it needs to be supplemented with a logic of the description of action before it can become genuinely practical; and that in order to become an imperative logic it needs to incorporate features to take account of the difference between fiats and directives. Moreover, it fails to represent adequately something which is intuitively of great importance in practical reasoning: the weighing up of the pros and cons of a particular course of action. Where an agent's goals are consistently realizable, then the consideration of the advantages and disadvantages of particular actions can be seen as the search for a conclusion-fiat derivable from a goal-fiat which will incorporate all the ends which provide the standards of advantageousness and disadvantageousness for the case in point. But there is no guarantee that the ends are capable of joint attainment, and in such a case what is needed is not a refinement of the Aristotelian end-means reasoning, but something more like contemporary decision theory.

But though the logic of satisfactoriness is only a part of the logic of practical reasoning, it is a central part. The justification for concentrating on it almost exclusively in the present chapter is that the crucial characteristic of defeasibility which it displays will be preserved in any richer logic of which it forms a part. And it is this feature, as I hope to show, which is the feature of practical reasoning most intimately connected with the freedom of the will which is our principal concern.

VI

BETWEEN REASON AND ACTION

The conclusion of a piece of practical reasoning, it is often said, is an action. In support of this statement the authority of Aristotle is commonly cited. In the *De Motu Animalium* there occurs the following passage:

> (In practical reasoning) the two premisses result in a conclusion which is an action—for example, one thinks that all men are to march and that one is a man oneself: straightway one marches; or no men are to march now and that one is a man: straightway one halts. And so one acts in the two cases provided that there is nothing to compel or to prevent. Again, I should make a good thing, a house is a good thing: straightway I make a house. I need a covering, a cloak is a covering; I need a cloak. What I need I should make, I need a cloak; I should make a cloak. And the conclusion—'I should make a cloak' is an action. And the action goes back to the beginning or first step. If there is to be a coat, one must first have B, and if B then A, so one gets A to begin with. That the action is the conclusion is clear. (701a7 ff.)

The passage is not free from ambiguity. Though Aristotle twice speaks as if the action itself (of walking, or halting, or getting A) was the conclusion of the reasoning, he also calls 'I should make a cloak'—which is a *description* of an action—'the conclusion'; he even calls it 'an action', which calls in question the sense of that word in the other passages. If he did think that the conclusion of a piece of practical reasoning must always be an action, he was surely wrong: as he says himself in this passage, something may intervene, after the conclusion of the practical reasoning, to prevent the performance of the action. Further, the conclusion of a piece of practical reasoning may be a decision about the future, which cannot be carried out until the time comes. Again, when we reason about what a historical figure should have done, or try to discover the reasons which made him act as he did, we are surely making use—*inter alia*—of the same patterns of inference as we are in reasoning which is practical in the strict sense of being geared to our own action. Perhaps all Aristotle means is that when our reasoning concerns actions to be performed immediately, there is no need to pause to draw the conclusion in words before getting on with the business in hand. But of course something similar holds of the premises as well as the conclusion of practical reasoning: as Aristotle himself says, a few lines further in the same passage, we don't waste time contemplating obvious premises such as 'I am a man'.

Whatever be the sense of this passage of Aristotle, the correct account seems to be that the conclusion of a piece of practical reasoning is a description of an action to be done: a fiat concerning the reasoner's action. As a fiat it is an expression of the reasoner's wants; as the conclusion of a piece of practical inference it is the output of his reason: it fits what Aristotle says in *Nicomachean Ethics VI* of *prohairesis* or choice: it is 'appetitive intelligence or ratiocinative appetite', depending on which way you look at it.

The description of action to be done which is the conclusion of practical reasoning furnishes a description under which the action, if performed, is intentional. What is done by the agent as the upshot of practical reasoning is action answering to the description given by the conclusion. There will always be indefinitely many different actions answering to any given description: actions which differ from each other in that different, incompatible, descriptions can be given of them. Thus, if the conclusion of a piece of practical reasoning is 'I am to open the door' there are many different actions—e.g. opening the door with the right hand, opening the door with the left hand, opening the door with a kick—which will answer to the description. An action, once performed, may be intentional under some of these descriptions (one or more than one) and not intentional under others.[1]

---

[1] The description under which what is done is intentional may be, as von Wright has emphasized, a conjunction or disjunction of 'atomic' act descriptions.

An agent must be aware of the description under which his acts are intentional: if he is φing intentionally, then he knows that he is φing. In saying this, I do not wish to rule out the possibility of unconscious intention. I do not wish to deny, that is, that there may be cases where a psychoanalyst may be in a better position than his patient to tell us what the patient's own intentions are. It may happen that a psychoanalyst and his patient both agree that a certain action is intentional under description X, but the psychoanalyst may affirm, and the patient deny, that it is also intentional under description Y; and in this case the psychoanalyst may be right and the patient wrong. Only, if we are to attribute intention at some level deeper than that of everyday consciousness, we must attribute awareness at the same level at which we attribute intention.

What I mean by differences of level is best brought out by considering some examples. Freud, in *The Psychopathology of Everyday Life*, quotes the case of a professor at Vienna who, in his inaugural lecture, instead of saying, according to his script, 'I have no intention of underrating the achievements of my illustrious predecessor' said 'I have every intention of underrating the achievements of my illustrious predecessor'. Freud regards the professor's slip of the tongue as a better guide to his intentions than the words he had written in his notes. But here the professor was perfectly well aware of his attitude to his predecessor's achievement; his intention was only 'unconscious' in the sense that he did not mean to *express* it in his inaugural. The utterance of 'every', on the other hand, was in the normal sense *un*intentional; Freud himself thinks it is intentional only in the sense of being revelatory of the *other* intention.

Consider a more complicated case. One of Freud's patients, an Austrian undergraduate, was staying at a holiday resort during the vacation. He was suddenly obsessed with the thought that he was too fat: he said to himself 'Ich bin zu dick'. Consequently, he gave up all heavy foods, and used to leap up from the table before the pudding arrived in order to run up mountains in the August heat. Later, during the analysis of the undergraduate, Freud reports: 'Our patient could think of no explanation of this senseless obsessional behaviour until it suddenly occurred to him at this time his fiancée had also been stopping at the same resort in company with an attractive English cousin called Dick.' His purpose in slimming, Freud suggests, had been to get rid of this Dick (X, 183).

This is not one of Freud's most plausible cases—but why his account is so implausible is not because the purpose (to get rid of Dick) is implausible but precisely because the belief (by slimming I am getting rid of Dick) it imputes is an incredible one involving a puerile pun.

In this case, both the patient and the psychoanalyst would agree that the patient's actions were intentional under certain minimum descriptions: e.g. I intend to leave the table before the suet dumplings arrive. The more interesting cases are those where the patient would deny that a certain action was intentional at all, under any description. The same patient, faced with the choice of marrying a poor girl whom he loved, and a rich one chosen by his parents, fell ill. Freud writes: 'The chief result of his illness was an obstinate incapacity for work, which allowed him to postpone the completion of his education for two years. But the results of such an illness are never unintentional; what appears to be the consequence of the illness is in reality the cause or motive of falling ill' (X, 189). 'Falling ill' is not the sort of thing which we normally regard as being intentional at all; yet we can imagine circumstances in which Freud's view could be made to look very plausible. Because here the knowledge 'I am unable to complete my education while ill' is to hand.

Cases of 'unconscious intention' are cases of a clash between the verbal expression (or lack of expression) and the manifestation of behaviour.[2] The expression of an intention in words is only a part of a whole pattern of behaviour which manifests an intention. Someone else can contradict one's expression of intention if it does not fit in with the rest of one's behaviour. It is true that a person has the last word on what his intentions are if by this we mean that it is *his* behaviour which is the criterion of what his intentions are, and not *our* beliefs about the possibility of his success. But he has not the last word on what his intentions are if by this we mean that what he *says* is to outweigh what he *does* as evidence for his true intentions. In other words, he alone

---

[2] It is when psychoanalytic writers attribute unconscious intention not on the basis of anything in the patient's actual behaviour, but on the basis of (unsubstantiated) theories about human nature in general that they forfeit credibility.

chooses the target at which he is aiming; but we will decide which target he is aiming at not only, and not even primarily, by what he says, but by which way he is facing and pointing.

Since a psychoanalyst, or a perceptive friend, may observe the agent's behaviour, they may often decide correctly what the agent's intentions are; and they may be correct even if the agent verbally denies these intentions. I do not mean that they may be in a better position to observe the agent's intentions than the agent himself is. The agent does not observe his own intentions; he *has* them. He may say that he has certain intentions when in fact he has other intentions; if this is so, then this is not an erroneous report of his observations, but an inconsistency in his behaviour, which may be more or less deliberate. If it is very deliberate, we shall say that he is deceiving others; if it is less deliberate we shall say that he is deceiving himself. No rigid boundary can be drawn between the two.

We can accept, therefore, the notion of unconscious intention without breaking the link between intentionality and practical reasoning. To attribute unconscious intention is *eo ipso* to attribute unconscious practical reasoning. The reasoning may be unconscious simply in the sense that it was not formulated, but could be without difficulty on demand; or it may be that it would be something which the reasoner would only explicitly formulate in private and in confidence; or something even which he might only be prepared to recognize as his own as a result of a more or less prolonged application of a therapeutic technique.

Whether the reasoning is conscious or unconscious in any of these ways, the connection between practical reasoning and action has an ineradicable looseness. The link between a reason and an action is loose in three different ways: first, the same reasons, occurring as premisses in a piece of practical reasoning, may legitimate different conclusions; secondly, different actions may each accord with the conclusion; thirdly, the conclusion may not be acted on at all—and that without the appearance of any interfering or preventing factor, as in the case of weakness of the will. The second of these features has already been considered: we must now say something about the first and the third.

It is a feature of practical reasoning that the same premisses may license different conclusions. Of course, in theoretical reasoning too more than one conclusion may be drawn from the same premisses. What is peculiar to practical reasoning is that different and *incompatible* conclusions may be drawn from the same premisses. My current desires and beliefs, set out as premisses in practical form, may equally license the conclusion that I should take the bus to London at 2.15, and the conclusion that I should take the train to London at 2.15; but taking the bus and taking the train are incompatible.

This seems to me an unavoidable, important, and by no means paradoxical feature of practical reasoning. Many philosophers have found it unacceptable: if practical reasoning can thus lead to opposite conclusions, they have argued, that means that the agent can have no sufficient reason for choosing one course of action rather than the other, and whatever course he finally chooses his actions will be inexplicable by his reasons. Thus Leibniz, and many philosophers before him and after him, concluded that a rational agent's actions will always be for the best. God will always do what is most perfect, and man will always do (though freely) what appears best (G IV 438).

Such a view makes it difficult to understand Leibniz's other, better inspired, maxim that reasons incline but do not necessitate. No good reason has ever been given for the view that a rational agent always acts for the best. If an agent does something because it will satisfy his purpose—assuming that the purpose is a sane one—he has a reason for doing what he does; his claim to have acted rationally is in no way weakened by the fact that there are other equally good or even better ways of achieving his purpose. The application of Leibniz's principle to God led to the conclusion that this is the best of all possible worlds, and one does not need to be Voltaire to find that conclusion incredible. The application of Leibniz's principle to human agents must leave them, in the multiple indifferent circumstances of everyday life, in the dilemma of Buridan's ass.

The final feature which loosens the links between practical reasoning and action is the phenomenon of weakness of will, that failure to act on the conclusion of practical reasoning which philosophers have called akrasia, or incontinence. It is moral backsliding that has been the principal object of study: failure to live up to one's moral beliefs and the conclusions they imply for one's actions. In the view of most men innocent of philosophy, this is a recurring feature of the lives of weak mortals like ourselves; but from the days of Socrates until our own times there have been philosophers reluctant to accept incontinence at its face value.

The plain man's view of incontinence is well expressed in a passage from Macaulay's essay on Sir James Mackintosh. Macaulay criticizes James II's folly in believing that the Tories, because they professed to consider resistance to the royal will as sinful, would support his plans for toleration. 'It might', he says, 'have crossed the mind of a man of fifty who had seen a great deal of the world, that people sometimes do what they think wrong . . . Only imagine a man acting for one single day on the supposition that all his neighbours believe all that they profess, and act up to all that they believe. Imagine a man acting on the supposition that he may safely offer the deadliest injuries and insults to everybody who says that revenge is sinful; or that he may safely entrust all his property without security to anyone who says it is wrong to steal. Such a character would be too absurd for the wildest farce.'

Philosophers have agreed with Macaulay that men do not always believe what they profess. But notoriously some have found difficulty in the statement that men do not act up to all that they believe. To anyone who accepts a prescriptivist ethic there is a paradox in the suggestion that men sometimes fail to do things which they can do, and think they ought to do, but do not want to do.

If to say that one ought to do a certain action is to prescribe the action to oneself and to others in like circumstances, how can a man fail to do what he thinks he ought to do, or do what he thinks he ought not to do? What a man does is a better guide than what he says to what he believes; if then a man says he ought to do something but does not do it, the prescriptivist must conclude that he does not really mean what he says, and is deceiving us, and possibly himself also, about his beliefs.

In his book *Freedom and Reason* R. M. Hare puts forward an answer to this difficulty. Human language being the language of weak mortals, he says, the meaning of the word 'ought' is such as to allow for weakness of will: language has built into its logic all manner of ways of evading the rigour of pure prescriptive universality. The word 'ought', it seems, has two senses: one when it is used with universal prescriptive force by a man prepared to obey his own prescriptions and another attenuated sense which is exploited by the backslider. In passing from the one sense to the other, however, there is no equivocation; it is part of the meaning of the word 'ought' that we are capable of backsliding.

The typical case of moral weakness, Hare thinks, involves an inability, in some sense, to do what we think we ought. An agent may make a moral judgement and find that it is not in his psychological power to act on the imperatives that are entailed by it. It is a tautology to say that we cannot sincerely assent to a command and at the same time not perform it, if now is the occasion for performing it and it is in our power to do so. But this does not present a difficulty for the interpretation of 'ought' as entailing imperatives, because 'nobody in his senses would maintain that a person who assents to an imperative must (analytically) act on it even when he is unable to do so'. So it is possible to think that one ought to do something and yet not do it; namely when one *cannot* do it. 'Ought' in the fullest sense implies 'can'; so the 'ought' which remains is the downgraded one which we spoke of above.

We commonly express our disapproval for backsliders, and feel remorse for our own moral weakness; Hare maintains this is no objection to his view. Remorse and disapproval, though unable to overcome a particular temptation, may keep alive the will-power which may overcome lesser ones.

There are several difficulties in Hare's explanation. First, it seems that the proper course for the backslider that Hare describes would be to withdraw his prescription as soon as he becomes aware of his disability. For, on Hare's own account, a man cannot properly universally prescribe a course of action unless he assents to the prescription himself. But this the backslider cannot do. It is not that a man must act on an imperative, if he has assented to it, even though he is unable to do so. It is rather that, if he cannot act on it, he cannot sincerely assent to it. It is no good saying, 'Of course, I agree to do what you want, but unfortunately, I cannot *do* it, I can only agree to do it.' A man may sincerely assent to an imperative, and later find himself incapable of obeying it; but that is not the case Hare's account was meant to explain.

Second, the phrase 'psychological inability' calls for investigation. Are the man's wants to be taken into account as psychologically inhibiting factors, or not? If not, then the only things which he is psychologically unable to do, are the things which he will not do no matter how much we make it in his interest to do them, and no matter how much we try to deter him from leaving them undone. If the man who is psychologically unable to get up when he thinks he ought to is unable in this sense, then he will not get up even if his sheets are on fire. But this is more than weakness of will, this is paralysis. The compulsive neuroses which Hare offers as the clearest samples of 'psychological inability' I take to be cases of this kind.

But even in more normal cases of weakness of will, Hare maintains, 'in a deeper sense, the man cannot do the act'. This deeper sense of 'cannot' must be a sense which takes into account the man's wants. 'He cannot' must mean 'given his present desires, he cannot': i.e. the doing of this is incompatible with his present desires. But of course to say that a man cannot do something because he is prevented by his desires is just to say that he can do it, but won't because he doesn't want to; which was precisely the description of the state of affairs which set Hare a problem.

If a man is genuinely unable to fulfil some obligation through a psychological disability similar to a compulsive neurosis, there would seem little point in reproving him, and his feelings of self-reproach will be merely further evidence of his neurotic state. But if blame and remorse are pointless, punishment would be positively unjust. Yet people are punished not only for failing to have the right moral principles, but also for violating the moral principles which they have. On Hare's account, this seems difficult to justify.

Hare seems to me wrong in regarding the making of moral judgements as the issuing of a special type of imperative, but I have throughout accepted his comparison of wishes and desires to frames of mind which find expression in imperatives. I think that it is in this direction that we should turn for a solution of the paradox. The problem of moral weakness may be seen as a particular case of the problem of conflicting wants: for if there is something paradoxical about a man's failing to do something in his power which he sincerely says he ought to do, there should be something even more paradoxical about his failing to do something in his power which he sincerely says he wants to do. In each case he fails to act because he has another want incompatible with the fulfilment of his duty or his first want. When a man says that he ought to do something, he can always be asked 'under pain of what ought you to do it?' and the answer may be 'under pain of injustice, or unkindness, or folly', for example; and if he fails to do what he ought to do, this means that for the time being he wants something else more than he wants not to be unjust, or unkind, or foolish. But his failure in no way counts against his genuinely believing that his action is unjust, or whatever; and though it counts against, it is not altogether incompatible with his genuinely wanting not to be unjust. On other occasions, perhaps, he goes to great trouble to avoid injustice; and perhaps he would on this occasion also, were the pressure of the hindering desire removed.

Yes, it may be said, but that does not show that on *this* occasion he wants to be virtuous, nor does it show that on this occasion he *can* do the virtuous action. But this objection seems to depend on a misconception of the nature of wanting and ability. Neither wants nor abilities—nor, for that matter, beliefs—are events or processes which are tied to particular moments. Of course, wants, abilities and beliefs are attributed to people on the basis of the things which they say and do at particular times and in particular places; and it may be true of someone at a particular time and in a particular place that he can do such and such, that he wants such and such a thing, and that he has such and such a belief. But its being true of him then and there is not necessarily in virtue of anything which is happening then and there. For this reason it may be true of a man that at a particular time and place he wants something, even though what is happening then and there is such even as to count against his wanting it.

The want in such a case cannot be the man's strongest want, in the sense in which an agent's strongest want at any given moment is the want he is acting upon; but in another sense the backslider's volition to be virtuous may be a stronger want than the desire which is at present leading him to act viciously. For it may be a desire which governs a greater part of his behaviour and which lasts throughout his life; whereas his present vicious desire is a temporary aberration which will soon pass away.

If this is a correct account we can see more clearly *what* is weak in a case of weakness of the will. By 'the will' in this context cannot be meant simply the ability to want: if this were so, we might say that the incontinent man has a particularly strong will, since his violation of his principles is a tribute to the imperiousness of his momentary desires. Nor is it simply the ability to act for reasons, the incontinent may reason how to satisfy his lusts. No: as it figures in this discussion, the will is the faculty for giving effect in one's life to long-term projects and stable policies; and it is contrasted with the more instant and fluctuating desires which are intimately connected with bodily states and processes, such as hunger and thirst, the need for sleep and sex and the cravings for nicotine or alcohol. The man of strong will is the man who can prevent the short-term wants from interfering with the execution of the long-term volitions, either by refusing to satisfy them, or by planning their satisfaction at times and in manners which leave room for the pursuit of the dominant goals and permanently desired qualities. Strength of will in this sense is not directly a moral phenomenon; it is a necessary, but not a sufficient condition for a good life: it can be exercised in the pursuit of evil ends or indifferent purposes, and can minister to vices or neutral traits of character as well as to virtues.

Akrasia has often figured in discussions of freedom of the will. From one point of view, it may seem a paradigm exercise of freedom, providing a clinching counterexample to any assertion of psychological determinism: does it not show that however strong a man's reasons may be for choosing one of two alternatives he may go on in fact to choose the other? From an opposite point of view akrasia may seem to be a threat to freedom: surely there is something paradoxical in suggesting that a man is most free, when he is least in control of himself?

The account of the will thus far presented should incline us to sympathize with the second, rather than the first, of these reactions. If the will is the ability to act for reasons, then acting in the face of all one's reasons can hardly be the paradigm exercise of the will, even if it may be the most vivid demonstration of the existence of that ability to act otherwise which is a crucial element in the voluntary behaviour of a non-incontinent agent. But we can only see what justice there is in each of the reactions after we have given full consideration to the issue of psychological determinism, to the question whether a man's reasons or wants or beliefs are determining causes of his action.

When we ask whether reasons are causes, it is clear that the reasons which come into consideration are those which, in the sense earlier elucidated, present to a man's mind. The thinness of the ice around the island may be a very good reason for me not to skate too near it: but no one will claim that it will have any causal influence on my skating behaviour if I am quite unaware of it. The reasons which, if psychological determinism is true, cause my actions, are *my* reasons, the wants and beliefs which actually enter into my practical reasoning, the wants and beliefs which find expression in the fiats and statements which constitute the premisses from which I infer how I should act. The question whether reasons are causes is very intimately connected with the questions we have been raising about the nature of practical reasoning.

'It could hardly fail to be true', says David Pears in his paper 'Predicting and Deciding', 'that the agent's reason for his decision or action is a cause in some sense of that versatile word' (p. 121). This is undeniable. In the first systematic treatment of the concept of cause, that of Aristotle, the final cause appears along with the efficient, formal, and material cause, as one of the Four Causes: and one kind of final cause is the goal of a reasoning agent. But when we talk of causes nowadays it is commonly efficient causality we have in mind: and certainly in the context of a discussion of freedom and determinism the interesting question is whether reasons are efficient causes of action.

Aristotle's efficient causes were individual substances: a sculptor was the efficient cause of a statue, and a dog of a puppy. Since Hume most philosophers have come to think of causality not as a transaction between substances, but as a relationship between events and states. The agent-causality described by Aristotle is regarded as a special form of event-causality. What Davidson says with regard to human agency would be widely accepted as applying to agent-causality in general:

> An important way of justifying an attribution of agency is by showing that some event was caused by something the agent did. If I poison someone's morning grapefruit with the intention of killing him, and I succeed, then I caused his death by putting poison in his food, and that is why I am the agent in his murder ... The notion of cause appealed to here is ordinary event-causality, the relation whatever it is, that holds between

two events when one is cause of the other. For although we say
the agent caused the death of the victim, that is, that he killed
him, this is an elliptical way of saying that some act of the
agent—something he did, such as put poison in the grape-
fruit—caused the death of the victim. ('Agency' 10)

Following Hume, most philosophers have accepted further that as
a first approximation to stating the relation that must hold
between two events when one is the cause of the other we can say:
A causes B iff (a) it is logically possible for A to exist without B
and vice versa, (b) there is a non-trivial empirical generalization to
the effect that whenever there occur events of a type to which A
belongs there occurs a subsequent event of a type to which B
belongs. Since Mill most philosophers would further agree that
(c) the generalization must be stated in such a way as to allow for
the possibility of interference: it must either contain an express
proviso 'unless interference occurs' or, if possible, the types to
which A and B belong must be so specified as to include in their
description the ruling out of interfering factors.

When contemporary philosophers, then, raise the question
whether reasons are causes the question they commonly have in
mind is whether the relation between reason and action can be
brought into accordance with the basically Humean pattern just
sketched. It is this question to which I shall now turn.

If reasons are Humean causes, then in saying that an agent
acted as he did because of the state of his desires and beliefs, we
are saying that whenever that state of desires and beliefs recurs
in a similar situation, he will perform a similar action. The
Humean can of course admit that we are rarely, if ever, in a
position to detail exactly what is the state of desire and belief
adequate to ensure the performance of an action; but, he claims,
in saying that an action ϕ was performed *because of* the reasons
we are committed to saying that the reasons in the circumstances
constituted a sufficient antecedent condition of the action; that is
to say, that *some* description of the circumstances and the state
of desire and belief can be given such that there is a true covering
law to the effect that any human being so circumstanced in a
state answering to that description performs an action answering
to the description 'ϕ'.

Anti-Humean writers have claimed that it is of the essence

of rational action that *no* such generalization be able to be given. Thus Geach has argued that the difference between natural and voluntary causality can be brought out as follows.

> If a physical description of some set-up is given, we cannot coherently say that an effect E *and* the opposite effect would equally fulfil the tendencies involved in that set-up. Now for contrast let us consider . . . action after deliberation. However carefully we describe a man's weighing of the pros and cons, we may end the story with 'and then he did it' or with 'and then he didn't do it' and *equally* make sense, equally have shown what led up to the man's action. In scholastic language, natural tendencies are one-way, *ad unum*: voluntary tendencies are two-way, *ad utrumque*. Of course if the man did it we shall say he did it because of the pros and in spite of the cons, and vice versa, if he didn't do it—but either story will be a coherent account. ('The Will', 2, 6–7)

A Humean might agree with Geach that either story—in the pages of a novel, say—will equally make sense. But this, he would say, shows no more about reason than science fiction shows about natural causality. If there are, as the Humean claims, covering laws governing behaviour, then stories of agents acting clean in the face of the reasons must either depend on inadequate statements of the operative reasons, or be mere pieces of science fiction —social-science fiction.

The Humean will of course agree that agents do often act against reason and perform actions different from those that would naturally be predicted from their patent desires and beliefs. But this, he will say, is merely a case of interference, a phenomenon which is equally familiar in the case of natural causality. The phenomenon has been well described by Geach himself in another context:

> Any alleged uniformity is defeasible by something's interfering and preventing the effect; to assert the uniformity as a fact is to commit oneself to a rash judgement that such interference never has taken place and never will. Scientists do not try to describe natural events in terms of what always happens. Rather, certain natural agents—bodies of certain natures—are brought into the description, and we are told what behaviour

is proper to this set of bodies in these circumstances. If such behaviour is not realised, the scientist looks for a new, interfering agent that has not so far been brought into the account . . .

Mill was correct to say that 'All laws of causation, in consequence of their liability to be counteracted, require to be stated in words affirmative of tendencies only.' Geach continues:

It is clear from the context that Mill's use of 'tendency' here has nothing to do with what usually happens; for he says that *all* heavy bodies *tend* to fall, although balloons do not usually fall. Similarly, he is not speaking of what is likely to happen; for, to take another of his examples, there is not the least likelihood that a one-ton pull will raise a body weighing three tons. A tendency is indeed specifiable, always and exclusively, by describing what happens if the tendency is fulfilled; but not all tendencies do pass to fulfilment . . . Given the natural agents involved, we know their tendencies; given all the tendencies involved, we know what will actually happen. (Thus, given the members of a structure, we know what stresses will be set up; and given all the stresses, we know what deformations will be produced.)

Geach may be right that Mill's tendency account of causality is not a modification of, but something entirely incompatible with, Hume's invariable succession theory; but this point is not important when we are trying to evaluate the claim of a modern follower of Mill and Hume that reasons are causes, and that failures to act in the manner to which the reasons point is an instance of the same kind of interference as we meet with in dealing with the non-rational causal operation of natural agents.

A sophisticated contemporary follower of Hume, David Pears, in his paper 'Rational explanation of actions and psychological determinism' presents a version of psychological determinism which offers ample room for the intervention of interfering factors between reason and action. Rational explanations of actions, he concedes, do not presuppose psychological determinism, but they do point in the direction of determinism. They have a structure which resembles the structure of physical causal explanation, and the structure is capable of being improved by being made less loose: and it is determinism which provides the focal point which fixes the direction of the lines of improvement. If an agent states that he did A only in order to achieve B, he implies that at similar points in his history he will perform a similar action. But this general implicate needs qualification.

> It is not implied that the desires mentioned by the agent are sufficient to lead to a similar action whenever an opportunity is presented, but only when they have not decreased in number or in strength in the interim, and only when there is no new opposition either from desires or from factors other than desires. (p. 110)

The 'opposition from desires or from factors other than desires' is meant to be handled, no doubt, as a species of interference parallel to the cases mentioned in Mill's examples.

In order to show that rational explanations have the same structure as ordinary causal explanations of physical events, Pears argues that they are open to the same kind of falsification by negative instances.

> An agent may say 'I did A only in order to achieve B' or he may say 'I would not have done A unless I had wanted to achieve B'. The first of these two statements implies that the desire mentioned was sufficient to lead to the action without any other desires . . . The statement 'I did A only in order to achieve B' entails its counterfactual contrapositive 'If I had not done A I would not have wanted to achieve B'. But this hypothetical is not directly testable, and so, if we want to test the sufficiency-implication of the agent's original statement we shall have to look further afield and see what happens at other points in his history.

To test the hypothetical we need to ensure that the desire is specified in a sufficiently general way, and to take precautions against a test being ineffective because of a change in the pattern of desires or the emergence of interfering factors. 'If this account of the structure of rational explanations of actions is correct' Pears says 'it is easy to see how it is related to psychological determinism. If the structure is to become deterministic it only needs to be improved in a few obvious ways' (p. 100).

Unfortunately, the argument quoted above begs the question of psychological determinism from the start. If an agent says 'I did A only in order to achieve B' he implies that the aim of achieving B was his only *reason* for doing A. But unless we assume that 'reason' is equivalent to 'antecedent condition sufficient in the circumstances to produce action' we cannot go on to infer that 'the desire mentioned was sufficient to lead to the action without any other desires' or that if the agent had not done A he would not have wanted to achieve B. But the equivalence between 'reason' and 'sufficient antecedent condition' is the *thesis* of psychological determinism; not an uncontentious premiss which can be used to establish a version of that doctrine. Unless some form of psychological determinism is presupposed, what earthly reason is there for believing that 'I scratched only to get rid of the itch' entails 'Whenever I have an itch I scratch' or 'If I had not scratched, I would not have wanted to get rid of the itch'?

No doubt a resolute determinist will insist that if, on one occasion I itch and scratch, and on the other occasion I itch and do not scratch, there must be some difference between the two occasions: a desire to observe the *convenances*, say, present on the second occasion and not on the first, and conflicting with the raw desire to be rid of the itch. Well, it may be so; and again it may not; experience suggests that itches are sometimes followed by scratching and sometimes not, without there having to be a positive contrary desire one could put a name to in the cases where one itches without scratching. 'But in that case the itches can't be as intense as in the case when you scratch.' Do we have a method of measuring the intensity of itches then, independently of whether they lead to scratching? 'Not yet, maybe; but we will when the physiology of itching is better understood.' Perhaps: but all of this shows at best how the phenomena can be fitted into the thesis of determinism; it does not offer a reason for accepting that thesis.

Of course it is true that we often do test the genuineness of claims of the form 'I did A only for the sake of B' by watching to see what the claimer does on other occasions. If a city coun-cillor, voting on an issue in a way which furthers his own business prospects, claims to be motivated only by the public interest, we are unlikely to accept his say-so without qualms until we have seen how he votes when his private interests and the public interest are lined up on opposite sides. But the reason for this is that the example concerns an issue of moral principle—as, of course, do most of the real-life examples in which we try to sift people's motives. Now since moral principles are universal, one's actions in morally similar situations are a test of one's sincerity in claiming to be acting upon a moral principle on a particular occasion. But that is because of the nature of morality, not because of the nature of volition as such. Not everything that is wanted—not even everything that is rationally wanted—is wanted on principle. Consequently, if I say 'I scratched only to get rid of the itch' it in no way impugns my sincerity if you can point to other episodes in my biography when I itched without scratching, in the absence of interfering factors.

But though the concept of interference may be gratuitously introduced to shore up a deterministic thesis adopted on quite different grounds, it does seem to be the appropriate one to apply in a number of cases in which reasoning and action fail to accord Obviously, the actions of a rational agent like those of any other agent, can be prevented by external forces; but talk of interference seems also appropriate when an agent's own physical condition prevents him from acting as he wishes—when a climber, for instance, is determined for good reason to keep tight hold of a rope, but eventually finds his grip loosening against his will. These cases are not contentious: the more interesting question is whether the case of akrasia is sufficiently similar to the uncontentious cases for talk of interference to be appropriate there also.

Aristotle seems to take this view in his treatment of incontinence in Book VII of the *Nicomachean Ethics* (1174a31 ff.),[3] and even more clearly in Book II of the *Eudemean Ethics* (1224a32 ff.). In the incontinent man, reason suffers force from animal desire; it is prevented by desire from leading on to action. The incontinent man himself, for Aristotle, is not the victim of constraint, nor does he suffer any 'psychological disability'; for both the desire and the reason are *his*; taken as a whole, he acts willingly. But Aristotle uses the same vocabulary for the action of desire on reason as he does for the activity of an interfering external cause. In the case, then, of akrasia Aristotle makes use of the same concept as the Humean determinist.

This seems to me correct in the case which Aristotle takes as the

---

[3] I have discussed Aristotle's account at length in *The Anatomy of the Soul*, 28 ff.

paradigm of akrasia: where there is a conflict between a conclusion reached by reason and the operation of a blind, unreasoning, animal desire. The reason why it seems appropriate is that the tendencies which are in conflict are straightforwardly capable of separate identification because in each case we know what counts as a fulfilment of the tendency: the practical reasoning, *ex hypothesi*, has reached a specific conclusion; and the animal desires are identified as tendencies for immediate gratifications of familiar kinds.

But as we move away from the archetypal conflict of reason and animal desire the language of interference becomes less and less appropriate because the conflicting tendencies become less and less capable of independent specification. This is already the case in two other types of akrasia both mentioned by Aristotle—the case of impetuousness, where the animal desire prevents the practical reasoning reaching a conclusion (1150b22), and cases such as anger where what disaccords with the voice of reason is something which itself makes use of rational descriptions and concepts (1149a33). The reason for regarding the concept of interference as inappropriate here can best be appreciated if we consider the case where its application is even more inappropriate, namely, where the 'interference' is between reasons for and against a course of action.

Earlier in the chapter, I stressed that one, and the most important, way in which the connection between reason and action was loose is the defeasibility of practical reasoning. That is to say, a pattern of reasoning which would justify a certain course of action would cease to justify it if further wants and beliefs were brought into consideration, if further fiats and statements were added to the premisses of the practical reasoning. Now this phenomenon of defeasibility has to be dealt with by the Humean psychological determinist as one more case of interference: the new premisses which make the conclusion no longer derivable have to be treated as expressions of factors which interfere causally with the causal effectiveness of the wants expressed by the original premisses.

Because of the defeasibility of practical reasoning, there can be no generalizations of the form: 'Anyone who accepts such and such practical premisses must under pain of inconsistency accept such and such a practical conclusion' or 'Anyone who has such and such beliefs and desires must under pain of inconsistency act in such and such a manner'. The best generalizations we can hope to reach will have as their antecedents 'Anyone who accepts such and such practical premisses *and no others* . . .' and 'Anyone who has such and such beliefs and desires *and no others* . . .'.

The Humean will accept this, and say that the 'and no others' stipulation is parallel to the 'if not interfered with' stipulation in the physical case. But the parallel breaks down for the following reason: to give an account of a situation in terms of causal tendencies interfering with each other, you have to be able to give in advance an account of the action of the causal agent if not interfered with. Thus, to take an example given by Mill in his discussion of the composition of causes 'the expansive force of the gases generated by the ignition of gunpowder tends to project a bullet towards the sky, while its gravity tends to make it fall to the ground'—given these two tendencies, one can predict the actual trajectory of the projectile. But in the case of the factors supposed operative when reasons are considered causes—namely, wants and beliefs—there is nothing parallel at all.

Suppose that an agent, deliberating, holds in his hands a substance that he believes is poisonous. What tendency to action does this belief have, considered in isolation from the other factors which may be thought to combine with it in a mental parallelogram of forces? The answer is surely: none whatever. Of course, in combination with other factors (e.g. wants) it may lead to tendencies to act: coupled with the wish to protect his two-year-old son it may give rise to the tendency to put it out of the infant's reach; coupled with the wish to dispose of the brat as soon as possible, it may give rise to the tendency to put it into the infant's porridge. But neither of these tendencies can be regarded as being the result of an interference between a want and a belief.

But if not beliefs, surely wants are tendencies which can conflict? Well, certainly there can be conflicts between wants, in the sense that there may be situations in which any action which would lead to the satisfaction of one want will lead to the frustration of the other. But fortunately, such cases are comparatively rare and are certainly not the standard situation in which practical reasoning is brought to bear. On the contrary, the normal employment of practical reasoning is to ensure the harmonious satisfaction of a number of different wants in such a way that they do not conflict. The addition of an extra fiat to the premisses of a piece of practical reasoning need not mean that the other fiat-premisses cannot be satisfied; even in the case where this defeats the original pattern of practical reasoning, it need only mean that some other conclusion must be reached if the now augmented set of fiats is to be satisfied in its totality: as when, in the simple example considered earlier, the desire to work on the way to London was added to the desire to be in London by 4.15. The successful conclusion of a piece of practical reasoning, when put into action, means that all the wants are satisfied: they are *all* tendencies that have been fulfilled. Whereas when there is interference between causal tendencies, *none* of them are fulfilled, though what happens is the result of all of them.[4]

There is, then, a serious difficulty in regarding reasons as causes: we do not seem to be able to state the appropriate causal laws in the form of generalizations of tendency allowing for interference. There is another difficulty, which concerns not the second but the first element in the Humean notion of cause: namely, the separate identity, the logical separability, of cause and effect. This difficulty is a real one, but not easy to state accurately.

The connection between a want and its execution, it is sometimes said, cannot be a causal one because it is a logical one: it cannot be inductively established, because it is an *a priori* truth. The claim is a confused one, but contains a correct insight. The *a priori* truth is that wants are specified and identified by their fulfilments: in order to know what wanting to ϕ is you must know what ϕing is; the desire to ϕ differs from the desire to ψ precisely to the extent that ϕing differs from ψing; and so on. But this conceptual connection need not conflict with a causal connection. Don Locke has well said:

The fact that we call the particular want 'the want to do x' no more shows that it cannot be causally related to my doing x, than the fact that we call a certain smell 'the smell of coffee'

---

[4] Geach is rightly scornful of Mill's muddled pretence that what actually happens may be the sum of non-existent fulfilments of tendencies: so that if nothing happens at all, the nothing may be the sum of equal and opposite actual effects (*Three Philosophers*, 10).

shows that it cannot be causally related to coffee. . . . The mere fact that a want is described or identified or even defined by reference to some action no more shows that the action must, with logical necessity, follow upon that want than the fact that the smell is described, identified, even defined, by reference to coffee shows that coffee must, with logical necessity, be present where the smell is. Coffee and the smell of coffee are, in Hume's terms, distinct existences: one can occur without the other, and that, it seems is all that is required for 'Humean' causation. ('Reasons, Wants and Causes', 174–5)

The difficulty with regarding wants as Humean causes of action is not that where there is a want there must, of logical necessity, be the action; it is rather, as Locke goes on to argue, 'that wants and actions appear not to be distinct existences which might be connected by constant conjunction in the way Hume describes' (ibid., 176).

Those who regard reasons, wants, and beliefs as causes frequently treat them as mental events causally related to the physical events which are our actions. But it is incorrect to think of wants as mental events which determine action. To say that someone did an act because he wanted to is not to postulate a mental event as causing the action through some spiritual mechanism whose operation is as yet imperfectly understood. Some wants, of course, *are* mental events: pangs of hunger, pricks of lust or sudden impulses to pluck a flower. None the less, the wanting which makes an act voluntary, the wanting which makes the difference between voluntariness and non-voluntariness, is not as such a mental event. When, in philosophical discussion, I first uttered the sentence I have just written I uttered it voluntarily; I chose each word of it; yet there was no mental event of desiring to utter the word, no act of will distinguishable from the utterance of the word itself. And if some voluntary events—such as saying 'difference'—do not demand a specific event to cause them, why should any?

Locke himself argues that to want to do something is simply to have reasons (by which he means beliefs and items of knowledge) which actually incline one to act: my wanting to do something is not part of the cause of my doing it but consists simply in the fact that some reason does cause, or lead me to do it. The real cause of a person's actions are his beliefs: his wanting consists simply and solely in the fact that these beliefs influence his behaviour (ibid., 176).

Locke's view seems to me to give wants too little substantiality just as the view he attacks gave too much. His view might be plausible if each belief could find expression in only one action. But in fact we have different beliefs combined with the same want, and the same belief combined with different wants: we have to allow for beliefs and wants to be independent explanatory factors if our explanation is to have the same multiplicity as what is to be explained. It is obvious, Locke says, that a belief that the house is on fire can move people to action. Certainly: but it will depend on what they want *which* action they take—whether they rush out of the house, or rush into the house, or, like Nero, just reach for their fiddle.

Locke is right that there need be no mental event identifiable as a want, and in that sense no distinct existence capable of entering into a Humean relation of constant conjunction. But he is wrong to suggest that a want is never something separately identifiable, and he is wrong to identify wanting with the causal efficacy of beliefs. A belief seems a stronger candidate than a want for being a 'distinct existence': my wanting to utter the word 'difference' on a particular occasion may be indistinguishable from my uttering it as I did; but surely the same cannot be said of my knowledge that it has the meaning it has. But this contrast depends on the choice of examples of the content of the wanting and the belief: my belief that my wife is in earshot may find expression only in my talking to her: the sentence 'my wife is in earshot' need not form itself in my imagination at any point, nor need I have a more precise belief about exactly where she is. My belief that there is another step may simply be my lurching forward when arriving at the landing: nothing has to be going on in my imagination to make true the statement 'I thought there was another step'. Like wants beliefs may, but need not, be items of biography distinguishable from what they explain.

We can say, then, of beliefs and of wants that neither of them have to be an existence separate from the action they explain, in the sense of being separate events in the agent's biography. And since each of them can find expression as premises of practical reasoning, beliefs and wants are equally disqualified, in virtue of the defeasibility of practical reasoning, from figuring in causal generalizations of the appropriate structure to figure in Humean causal explanations.

It might be thought that the argument so far only shows that beliefs and wants are not necessarily separate events; but that this is quite inadequate to show that they are not causes. It may readily be granted that beliefs and wants are states, not events: but in the case of physical causation we regard states, such as the presence of oxygen, or the icy condition of the road, as causal factors no less than events.

To this I reply that beliefs and wants are indeed mental states, but not causally explanatory ones. To say that an agent brought about a certain result because he wanted to is certainly to say something about the causation of the result: but not that the action was caused by a certain mental state, but that the agent was free from certain types of causal influence, such as constraint. For an agent to have ϕd because he wanted to it is enough that (a) he knowingly ϕd, (b) he wanted to ϕ, (c) it was in his power whether to ϕ or not to ϕ.[5] There is no need to look for some mysterious causal link between the volition and the action. The state of the agent which makes his action voluntary is not a state which is linked by an imperfectly understood correlation to actions of this kind. On the contrary, it is a state which involves openness between performing or failing to perform the action. If there were a causal link between the want and the action, the action would cease to be voluntary. It may be that there is a causal generalization to the effect that those who have been without food for n days cannot help grabbing the first food they see, irrespective of all consideration for others. If so, there is a good case for saying that their movements are causally determined by their hunger. *Eo ipso*, they cease to be voluntary actions. In the normal case of motivated action this is not so. A man who gives a present out of generosity is not compelled to give by anything, not even by his generosity. The voluntary actions of an agent are not caused by anything, neither by the agent's desires, nor by the agent himself. The movements of his limbs and muscles as he goes about his business no doubt have their own causes: but that is a different matter.

In order to understand the relationship between reason and

[5] 'Want' is to be taken broadly, to include consent (cf. pp. 59, 118).

action, therefore, rather than pursue the will-o'-the-wisp of psychological determinism, we need to make a serious investigation of the concepts of ability, opportunity, and power. To this the next chapter will be devoted.[6]

[6] By rejecting psychological determinism I subscribe to what Donald Davidson has called 'the anomalousness of the mental'. Davidson himself accepts that reasons are causes: to say an action is intentional is precisely to say it was caused by the beliefs and wants that 'rationalize' it. But the causation is, in a manner of speaking, oblique: we cannot form law-like generalizations connecting agent's beliefs and desires with the acts they cause; instead, the beliefs and desires are identical with physiological events and states which are related by laws to the physiological events which are identical with the actions. No psycho-physical laws can be stated, however, relating physiological events of certain kinds with psychological events of certain kinds. ('Mental Events', in *Experience and Theory*.) Davidson's view leads, as he admits, to an insurmountable difficulty:

> Beliefs and desires that would rationalize an action if they caused it in the *right* way—through a course of practical reasoning, as we might try saying—may cause it in other ways. If so, the action was not performed with the intention that we could have read off from the attitudes that caused it. What I despair of spelling out is the way in which attitudes must cause actions if they are to rationalize the action.
>
> Let a single example serve. A climber might want to rid himself of the weight and danger of holding another man on a rope, and he might know that by loosening his hold on the rope he could rid himself of the weight and danger. This belief and this want might so unnerve him as to cause him to loosen his hold, and yet it might be the case that he never *chose* to loosen his hold, nor did he do it intentionally. ('Freedom to Act', 163)

Davidson admits very frankly that he does not know how to 'eliminate wrong causal chains'. But the difficulty is greater than he seems to see. For given his view, it is hard to see how causal chains can even be identified as 'wrong'. One *physiological* causal chain is as good as any other— each accords with physiological laws. It is no good saying that one of the causal chains corresponds, as the other does not, with the links between steps of practical reasoning; because even in the normal case such correspondence would be impossible unless there were psychological laws of the kind Davidson rejects.

VII

SPONTANEITY, INDIFFERENCE, AND ABILITY

Throughout the history of philosophy there have been two contrasting methods of expounding the nature of human free will. One approaches free will via the notion of wanting: we are free in doing something if and only if we do it because we want it. It is this approach which we have hitherto investigated, discussing in detail the type of want and the type of 'because' involved. The other method approaches free will via the notion of power: we are free in doing something if and only if it is in our power not to do it: to act freely is to act in possession of the power to act otherwise. There are traditional names for these two contrasting concepts of freedom: freedom defined in terms of wanting is liberty of spontaneity; liberty defined in terms of power is liberty of indifference. English philosophers are acquainted with the terms at least from the pages of Hume, who urges us to distinguish 'betwixt the liberty of spontaneity, as it is call'd in the schools, and the liberty of indifference; betwixt that which is oppos'd to violence, and that which means a negation of necessity and causes' (*Treatise*, III, II, II). The terms, as Hume indicates, are scholastic ones. Whether or not Hume was right to say that in his day 'liberty of indifference' *meant* a negation of causes, the expression was originally defined in terms of ability and opportunity; if it was taken to exclude causation, that was a conclusion, not part of the definition. But Hume is right that only liberty of indifference presents even a prima facie contrast with determinism; the contradictory of spontaneity is not determinism but compulsion. The two types of liberty appear to be distinct and in theory separable. If Descartes is right, a man with a clear and distinct perception of what he should do enjoys liberty of spontaneity without liberty of indifference; if Heisenberg is right some elementary particles are free from determinism without enjoying liberty of spontaneity.

The doctrine of liberty of indifference was first propounded in detail in the course of theological debates about freedom and predestination in the sixteenth century. The foremost exponent of the concept was the Spanish Jesuit Luis Molina, who defined freedom (liberty of indifference) in the following terms:

> An agent is free if, given all necessary conditions for øing, it both can ϕ and can not ϕ.[1]

Here the necessary conditions constitute the opportunity for øing: the 'can' refers to a two-way power or ability. In the present chapter I propose to discuss the 'can's of ability and opportunity with a view to evaluating the doctrine of liberty of indifference and relating it to the earlier discussion of liberty of spontaneity.

The first philosopher systematically to study the senses of 'can' and the different types of possibility was Aristotle. He drew various distinctions between kinds of potentiality and power which were later systematized by the scholastics. Active powers (e.g. the power to heat) differ from passive powers (e.g. the power to be heated); some powers (such as the senses) are innate while others (like the ability to play the flute) are acquitted by practice. The liberal and other arts which are the fruits of education belong to a particular class of powers: *hexeis*, *habitus* or 'dispositions'. These are powers whose exercises are the relevant scientific artistic and craft activities; but they are themselves actualizations of the capacity to learn which is presupposed by education. They can thus be called actualizations as well as potentialities: first or primary actualizations, as the scholastics said, codifying Aristotle, in comparison with the secondary actualizations constituted by the episodic employment of one's acquired skill. Thus the ability to speak Greek is a first actualization, the actual utterance of a bit of Greek, or the understanding of a particular Greek text, is a secondary actualization.

Of the distinctions which Aristotle drew between types of powers there is one of particular importance for our present concerns: the distinction between rational and irrational powers. He wrote:

---

[1] *Id liberum dicimus quod positis requisitis ad agendum in potestate ipsius habet agere aut non agere* (*Concordia Liberi Arbitrii* 14, 13d2).

Since some things can produce movement rationally and have the power of reasoning, and since the former powers must be in living things, whereas the latter may be in both animate and inanimate beings, it is necessary in the case of nonrational powers that when an agent and a patient are brought together the action and affect take place, whereas in the case of rational powers this is not necessary; for every one of the nonrational powers can have but a single effect, whereas the rational can have contrary effects, so that if they were under the same necessity as are the rational they would have contrary effects at the same time. But this is impossible. It is necessary, accordingly, that something else be decisive in rational action; I mean wanting or deliberate choice. (*Metaphysics* 1048a3 ff., trans. Hope, slightly adapted)

It is not clear from this passage whether the distinction between rational and nonrational powers is meant to coincide exactly with the distinction between one-way and two-way powers. This is a topic we have already encountered, and one to which we shall have to return. But if what we have said in the previous chapter was correct, Aristotle is right in locating wanting as the deciding factor in the exercise of two-way powers.

The Aristotelian apparatus of hierarchies of actuality and potentiality, the distinctions between different kinds of power, and indeed the very notion of power itself has been for centuries an object of contempt among philosophers. In recent times the distinctions have once again been studied—often quite independently of the scholastic background—and the hostility to the notion of power has been seen to rest on misunderstanding. One valuable, but misleadingly titled, contribution to this study is Michael Ayers' book *The Refutation of Determinism*.

In chapter four of his book Ayers identifies three distinct misconceptions of power: transcendentalism, scepticism, reductionism. The transcendentalist regards power as an occult entity ('How odd' he might think 'however quickly we lift the bonnet we are never able to see the horsepower'). This view far from doing justice to the reality of powers obscures the difference between judgements like 'this is red' and 'this can lift ten tons'. We don't observe powers, Ayers says, quite as we observe colours; for even if observing that a car is doing 100 mph is finding out that it can, simply observing that it is not doing 100 mph does not constitute finding out it cannot.

At the opposite extreme from the transcendentalist we can set the sceptic about powers. The sceptic thinks that none of the evidence for the ascription of power (past performance of an agent, performance of its fellows, future observation and future tests of the agent itself or its fellows) is adequate to give knowledge that power exists.

Finally, there is the reductionist. Developing Ayers' account, we might divide reductionists into two classes. For the one kind of reductionist power is nothing but its exercise; for another a power is nothing but its vehicle.[2]

Both transcendentalism and reductionism can exercise a powerful fascination on the mind. The later Wittgenstein devoted considerable energy to exhibiting the incoherence of transcendentalism. When doing philosophy, he wrote (PI 1 194), we sometimes have the thought: the possible movements of a machine are already there in it in some mysterious sense.

> What is this *possibility* of movement? It is not the *movement*, but it does not seem to be the mere physical conditions for moving either—as, that there is play between socket and pin, the pin not fitting too tight in the socket. For while this is the empirical condition for movement, one could also imagine it to be otherwise. The possibility of a movement is, rather, supposed to be like a shadow of the movement itself. But do you know of such a shadow? And by a shadow I do not mean a picture of the movement, for such a picture would not have to be a picture of just *this* movement. But the possibility of this movement must be the possibility of just this movement. (See how high the seas of language run here.) The waves subside as soon as we ask ourselves: how do we use the phrase 'possibility of movement' when we are talking about a given machine? But where did our queer ideas come from? Well, I show you the possibility of a movement, say by means of a *picture* of the movement 'so possibility is something which is like reality'. We say: 'it isn't moving yet, but it already has the possibility of moving—so possibility is something very near reality.' Though we may doubt whether such and such physical conditions make

[2] See above, page 10.

this movement possible, we never discuss whether *this* is the possibility of this or that movement; 'so the possibility of the movement stands in a unique relation to the movement itself; closer than that of a picture to its subject'; for it can be doubted whether a picture is the picture of this thing or that. We say 'Experience will shew whether this gives the pin this possibility of movement' but we do not say 'Experience will shew whether this is the possibility of this movement'—so it is not an empirical fact that this possibility is the possibility of precisely this movement'.

This was the sort of transcendentalism that Descartes and Molière attacked. Descartes declared Aristotelian qualities superfluous in the explanation of nature; Molière laughed at the Aristotelian doctors who explained that opium put people to sleep because it possessed a *virtus dormitivae.*

It was in reaction to transcendentalism that Hume declared that 'the distinction between a power and its exercise is entirely frivolous'. But reductionism had a history long before Hume. Aristotle found himself obliged to combat the Megarian doctrine that agents can ϕ when and only when they are actually ϕing (*Metaphysics Theta*).

If the Megarians are right, Aristotle says, then a ϕer is not a ϕer when he is not ϕing; for a person is not a ϕer if he can't ϕ. Thus the concept of 'art' or 'skill' disappears. Secondly, if ϕing is something that must be learnt, then every time the agent ϕs he learns to ϕ; and thus the concepts of 'learning' and 'forgetting' disappear. Thirdly, sense qualities will only exist when felt, and thus we shall reach a phenomenalist position. Fourthly, sense-powers will come and go with their operations: we shall be blind when we shut our eyes. Fifthly, if what is not ϕing cannot ϕ, and what cannot ϕ will not ϕ, no change at all will be possible. So, Aristotle concludes, we must make a distinction between power and its exercise, between act and potency; to remove this is to take away no small thing. We must conclude that it is possible that A is not ϕing but can ϕ and that A is ϕing but cannot ϕ.

Like Aristotle and Wittgenstein, Ayers tries to steer between reductionism and transcendentalism. His own positive account of powers makes a sharp distinction between natural and personal power which closely resembles the peripatetic distinction between nonrational and rational powers. Natural powers are capable of analysis in terms of subjunctive hypotheticals: with due qualification we can say 'A can do' means 'in some circumstances A would do'. The principal qualification to be made is that we must are to say that X can do A. Otherwise we shall have such countersay that certain *external* circumstances would *make* X do A, if we examples as 'If he says it will, it will', 'If it were a Rolls-Royce it would do 100 mph'. The distinction between extrinsic and intrinsic is difficult but unavoidable: we can see, for instance, that poor seed is not a *circumstance* of the failure of a crop, and that changing an engine is not a way of *testing* a car. When we test something, the antecedent which specifies the conditions of the test must be extrinsic, even though the consequence of a test may be an intrinsic change (like the explosion or dissolution of the thing to be tested). The notions of nature and of potentiality are conceptually linked: nature and powers cannot be sliced apart. 'A thing's powers characteristically constitute its nature, and indeed are largely responsible for our thinking of it as a thing with a nature at all.'

Ayers is surely right in seeing an essential connection between the notion of natural powers and the notion of testing. But there are many different types of test on the basis of which powers are attributed to agents. This was a matter to which Wittgenstein devoted considerable attention in *The Brown Book*, where several language games are constructed to illustrate the role of 'can'. The first three (a tribe who describe a board with a slot by saying 'this is a board in which the peg can be moved in a circle'; people who instead of saying 'the water is in the glass' say 'the water can be taken out of the glass'; people who say 'the house is built of sticks which can be bent easily') all describe different sorts of passive potentiality. Wittgenstein is principally interested in the different ways in which these are verified (in the first two we see the state described before our eyes: we see that the board has a circular slot, that the water is in the glass; in the third case, the state has no particular simultaneous sense-experience corresponding to it) (*The Blue and Brown Books*, 100–4).

Wittgenstein goes on to describe forms of active potentiality— a tribe who say 'a man can run fast' when we would say he has bulging leg muscles; who say 'a man can throw a spear' if he has passed certain other, unnamed tests before battle; or who—a different case—say 'he can do so and so' only if 'he has done so and so' is true (and not, e.g., if someone had done something more difficult). *The Brown Book* contains a lengthy discussion of these potentialities, especially mental potentialities, such as the one expressed by 'now I can go on' uttered by someone listening to the enunciation of a series (an example familiar to many readers from the *Philosophical Investigations*). The patient examination of the various types of criteria for the assigning of powers is meant to show the philosopher how to find his way between the opposite errors of transcendentalism and reductionism.

Much more than Wittgenstein, Ayers lays emphasis on the great difference between personal and natural powers. The powers of people, he argues, cannot be given a hypothetical analysis like the powers of things. But his arguments do not all carry conviction. If we are to give a hypothetical analysis of personal powers, he says reasonably enough, then one of the antecedent elements in the conditional must surely be the person's wants. He goes on

> Whatever we do mean by 'He can swim' it seems at least clear that if someone swims he can swim: p entails that p is possible. We do not also have to investigate the presence of a wish or the occurrence of a choice of effort nor the voluntariness of the swim, whatever that is. But how could we know that any conditional is true simply from knowing that its consequent is true? 'p' does not entail 'if q then p', or 'p only if q'.

This seems dubious on a number of grounds. It is, of course, of the subjunctive conditional, not the truth-functional 'if' that Ayers is talking about when he says that 'p' does not entail 'if q then p'. But could not the same point be made about natural powers—indeed did he not himself make a very similar point in the passage quoted above? This passage seems to put too much weight on the principle: if p then p is possible.

Ayers sums up his argument thus:

> I have argued that the ultimate verification of attributions of personal power, and of any proposition that some state of the agent or some set of circumstances in which he is placed is a

factor determining his ability to do an action is by reference to trials, that is, successes and failures; and that this verification cannot be explained on the model of stimulus-response or antecedent and consequent conditions; and that the difference between power and act corresponds to the difference between 'can I?' and 'shall I?'. (162)

But it is not clear how this settles the question of the relation between 'I can' and 'I will if I try'. It is surely true to say that if someone has the ability and opportunity to do X at t, and does his best to do X at t, then he will (normally do X at t. What makes the difference between such an ascription of personal power and the ascriptions of natural power is that the principle just enunciated, unlike 'if you set a match to it it will burn' is some kind of logical or conceptual truth and not a causal generalization linking two independent states of affairs. Trying to ϕ, it seems, is doing something with the intention of ϕing and without knowing whether one can ϕ or not; what one does, as Ayers points out, may simply be the action of ϕing itself, or a failure to ϕ.

The most important difference between natural powers and personal powers seems to be not so much that personal powers are not capable of conditional analysis as that wants are not circumstances. Perhaps this is Ayers' fundamental point. There are certainly some cases in which where only the want makes the difference between an action's being performed and its not being performed. But wanting is not a phenomenon to explain action in certain circumstances and not in others. Wanting in the relevant sense, we have argued, is defined by this sort of potentiality. The locus of wanting is precisely this gap between circumstances and action, the gap left by the unpredictability of action from circumstance. To say that an action is the result of a want, or is an exercise of a personal power, does not say anything about determinism; but it does say something about determinism by external factors. Personal powers are powers to do things when you want to: perhaps for this reason they are better called 'volitional powers' (for they belong also to animals: you can take a horse to the water but you cannot make him drink if he doesn't *want* to). A power is volitional only if there are no sets of external circumstances such that in those circumstances the agent will, necessarily, ϕ.

To attribute personal, or rather volitional, powers to an agent does not seem to involve saying that his actions are undetermined. Whether determinism is true or not the power to speak French is surely a volitional power. Of course, if we were in a position to control, via the brain, someone's lips and throat muscles so that French sounds came out, we would say that this was *not* evidence that he could speak French. But this is because the determining factor is an external agent, not because only indeterministically caused French is genuinely spoken French.

If volitional powers are not evidence in favour of indeterminism, this is not because (as some writers say) there might be circumstances which would necessitate the volitions of an agent and therefore necessitate action. If there could be such circumstances, then there would, by the definition just given, be no volitional powers. But the suggestion that circumstances—threats, say, or manipulation—might ensure action by necessitating volition misconceives the nature of volition. Wanting, to repeat, is not a phenomenon to explain action in certain circumstances and not in others; it is precisely defined by the gap between circumstances and action.

The relation between volitional power and determinism will be fully discussed in the next chapter. Before doing so, we must take much further the dissection of the senses of 'can' begun by Aristotle and revived by Wittgenstein and Ayers. It might be thought that this task would be greatly assisted by recent developments in the logic of modality. Many modal logics have been studied extensively in recent decades which can plausibly be offered as formalizations of the concepts of necessity and possibility which are used in logical and philosophical contexts (the 'alethic modalities'). Similar systems have been offered to incapsulate and explicate the intuitive notions of time, obligation, knowledge and belief: tense logics, deontic logics, epistemic logics, and doxastic logics. It might well be thought that one of the already available modal systems, or a closely analogous system, would provide a precise formalization of 'dynamic modality'[3]— a regimentation of the informal 'can' that we use in talking of the abilities and opportunities of human beings. This conjecture, I shall argue, is only partially correct.

In recent years philosophers and linguists have offered a

[3] The term is von Wright's (*An Essay on Modal Logic*).

number of distinctions between senses and uses of 'can' and between corresponding different types of possibility. Drawing on their work one can offer an incomplete list of ten distinguishable 'can's, which can be set out in the following table.[4]

Example	Type of possibility etc.	Type of modality
(1) (a) *Modus ponens* cannot lead from true premisses to a false conclusion (b) Nine can be divided by three (c) Equals can be substituted for equals	Logical or formal possibility	Alethic
(2) (a) Men cannot survive without oxygen (b) Smoking can cause cancer	Physical possibility; dispositions, natural powers	Dynamic
(3) (a) She can speak Russian (b) I can't touch my toes (c) Anyone can learn to drive a car	Ability, mental and physical powers; personal powers; human possibility	Dynamic
(4) (a) I couldn't cross the road (b) We can't expand the economy indefinitely	Circumstantial possibility; opportunity	
(5) (a) I could have sunk the putt (b) I was able to overtake the car	Particular possibility; 'all-in' can; natural possibility	
(6) (a) He can be very stubborn (b) You can't take a joke	Volitional possibility; character	
(7) (a) Can you pass the salt? (b) I could have slapped her face	Willingness, particular inclination	
(8) (a) I can hear a strange noise (b) I can't feel any pain	Perception and sensation	
(9) (a) Stonehenge could be a primitive computer	Epistemic possibility, consistency with known data	Epistemic
(10) (a) You can import one-fifth duty free (b) You can get down now (c) I cannot condone perjury	Legal, moral possibility	Deontic

[4] For the distinctions used in the table, see F. R. Palmer, *A Linguistic Study of the English Verb*; B. Aune, article 'Can' in *The Encyclopedia of Philosophy*; J. L. Austin, 'Ifs and Cans' in *Philosophical Papers*; P. Nowell-Smith, 'Ifs and Cans', *Theoria*, 1960; M. R. Ayers, *The Refutation of Determinism*; B. Gibbs, 'Real Possibility', *American Philosophical Quarterly*, 1970; A. M. Honoré, 'Can and Can't', *Mind*, 1964; J. P. Snyder, *Modal Logic and its Applications*; von Wright, *An Essay on Deontic Logic*.

Most if not all of these classifications reveal different senses of 'can': uses of 'can' in which different syntactical and semantical rules apply. Even within the ten different classes there are significantly different subclasses of instances, as the examples illustrate. Fortunately it is not a matter of present concern to investigate these differences in detail: the point of the table is to isolate by contrast the particular types of 'can' under discussion, the 'can' of opportunity and the 'can' which is used to report those human abilities, exercisable at will, of which the voluntary movements of the body and the speaking and thinking of units of language are the standard examples.

Some of the types of possibility which I have listed are capable of being confused with each other, and some of them are deliberately identified with each other by some philosophers. The possibilities most frequently confused or identified with ability are circumstantial and epistemic possibility, corresponding to the 'can' of opportunity and the 'can' of consistency with known data. There are, I think, good philosophical reasons for refusing the identification; but one does not need to be grinding a philosophical axe in order to draw the distinctions, and indeed in English they are clearly marked linguistically. The epistemic can —where 'it can be that p' is equivalent to 'For all we know to the contrary, p'—unlike the 'can' of opportunity or ability, is replaceable by 'may', and in British English usually is so replaced. The 'can' of ability and the 'can' of opportunity differ from each other in the way they form the future tense. 'I can speak Russian', in the present, according to context, may express either an ability or an opportunity. Not so in the future.

I can speak Russian tomorrow, we have guests coming from Moscow

is correct; but not

I can speak Russian next spring; I'm taking a beginner's course this fall.

The future of the 'can' of opportunity may be either 'I can' or 'I will be able'; the future of the 'can' of ability must be 'I will be able'. Similarly with conditionals. If an ability is attributed conditionally, it must be expressed by 'will be able' or the like; an opportunity can be attributed conditionally by the plain 'can'. Compare:

If you give me a hammer, I can mend this chair

with

If you teach me carpentry, I can mend this chair.

It is not difficult to see philosophical reasons for this and connected linguistic differences. A skill or ability is always a positive explanatory factor in accounting for the performance of an agent; an opportunity is often no more than a negative factor, the absence of circumstances that would prevent or interfere with the performance. Many abilities are states that are acquired with effort; opportunities are there for the taking until they pass. Whereas I have to possess an ability before I can exercise it, I may have an opportunity to do something which passes away before the time for taking it arrives: that is to say, it may be that now nothing prevents me from ϕing at t, but before t arrives something will have transpired to prevent me.

An ability is something internal to an agent, and an opportunity is something external. It is difficult to make this intuitive truth precise. The boundary between external and internal here is not to be drawn simply by reference to the agent's body: illness, no less than imprisonment, may take away the possibility of my exercising some of my abilities without necessarily taking away the abilities themselves. One thing that seems clear is that the presence or absence of an opportunity must be something external to an agent considered as a locus of current volition or wanting; of current decision, intention, choice and desire.[5] The mere lack of a desire to do something, the mere presence of a desire to do the opposite, does not by itself remove the opportunity to do it. I am away from home for three weeks and I fail to write to my wife: when I return home I can hardly avoid her reproaches by saying 'I had no opportunity to write: every time I had a spare moment I was prevented by a strong desire for a Martini.'

Abilities and opportunities are, of course, interconnected. Abilities can be exercised only when opportunities for their

[5] The effects of past volitions and desires may of course provide present constraints. But current desires—even in the case of an addict—do not remove opportunities; if the desires of an addict limit his liberty, they do so in some other way—perhaps by reducing his abilities.

exercise present themselves, and opportunities can be taken only by those who have the appropriate abilities. The greater one's ability the less one needs in the way of opportunity: a cliff which would be impossible of ascent for the normal person presents the skilled mountaineer with an opportunity for a good climb. Conversely, some opportunities may be so good that one needs no great ability to make use of them: if the ball is only 1 mm from the edge of the hole it will not take a very skilful golfer to sink the putt. In the limiting case, omnipotence needs no opportunities; or, to put it another way, omnipotence can make an opportunity out of anything. On the other hand, it does not seem that we can say that if an opportunity is good enough no ability at all will be needed to exploit it. The opposite pole from omnipotent ability seems rather to be the necessary exercise of natural powers, where what we have is not so much an opportunity for action as a sufficient condition for a reaction. Perhaps we should say that the realm of application of the two concepts of opportunity and ability coincides, with omnipotence and necessitation marking the extremes on either side.

There is an important difference between opportunities and abilities in relation to time. Opportunities are things which come and pass away; they are not like logical truths which remain for ever the same. Similarly, abilities come and go; what we are now able to do we may not always have been able to do and we may not always continue to be able to do.

Clearly, a full formulation of the logic of ability or opportunity would need to be combined with a tense logic, or a time logic, to allow for an indication of the time at which an opportunity occurred or during which an ability persisted. But the temporal modifications necessary in a logic of ability are simpler than those in a logic of opportunity.

In a logic of opportunity it is not only the opportunity-operator which needs to allow for temporal qualifications. Consider the following examples:

1 Now I can see you; a few moments ago I was busy, and couldn't
2 I can dine with you tomorrow, but not on Tuesday
3 Yesterday I could lecture on 5 May, today I can't (my engagement book has got filled up in the meantime)

In the first example the modality is temporally qualified but not the action; in the second the action is dated but not the modality; in the third, the action and the modality are both qualified but the temporal qualification of each is different. Clearly, an adequate formalization of opportunity-sentences will have to allow for independent dating of the sentences modalized and of the modalization. With the 'can' of ability no such double dating is necessary. The ability-operator needs temporal specification, but the description of the exercise of the ability should not be temporally specified. For abilities are inherently general; there are no genuine abilities which are abilities to do things only on one particular occasion. This is true even of abilities, such as the ability to kill oneself, which of their nature can be exercised only once.[6]

One might expect that the logic of ability and of opportunity might be easy to represent by a combination of a tense logic with some familiar modal logic (say, one of the Lewis system such as S_4 or S_5). With the logic of opportunity, this may well be so: I have argued elsewhere[7] that the system M (= Feys' system T), which can be regarded as the minimal alethic modal system, has a claim to represent the logic of opportunity, with a certain degree of artificial regimentation. But with the logic of ability it is not so. The two characteristic axioms of M are $CpMp$ (if something is the case, it is possible) and $EMApqAMpMq$ (the distribution of possibility over disjunction).[8] It is often claimed that these hold for ability. Consider $CpMp$ first. If I am speaking German, surely I can speak German. P. T. Geach, talking of concepts, has this to say in his book *Mental Acts*:

> To say that a man has a certain concept is to say that he *can* perform, because he sometimes *does* perform, mental exercises of a specifiable sort. This way of using the modal word 'can' is a minimal use, confined to a region where the logic of the word is as clear as possible. *Ab esse ad posse valet consequentia*

[6] For some ingenious but inconclusive arguments to the contrary, see Honoré, art. cit.

[7] In a paper 'The Logic of Ability' forthcoming in *Acta Philosophica Fennica*, on which part of the present chapter is based.

[8] In the Polish notation I use, 'M' is the weak modal operator; 'Mp' is to be read as 'Possibly p'. The strong modal operator 'L' is read: 'Necessarily p'.

—what is can be, what a man does he can do; that is clear if anything in modal logic is clear. (*Mental Acts*, 15)

But is it so clear? Perhaps, we may imagine, it is inconceivable that someone should speak a language without being able to speak it. In fact, it is quite often done. The late Pope Pius XII used to give audiences to American servicemen at the Vatican. The gracious speech which he delivered on these occasions had been composed, I was told, by an Irish monsignore and learned by heart under the coaching of an elocutionist. At those audiences the Pope spoke English; but he was not, in the normal sense, able to speak English.

The example may be contested (is such parroting really 'speaking English'?). But others are beyond dispute. A hopeless darts player may, once in a lifetime, hit the bull, but be unable to repeat the performance because he does not have the ability to hit the bull. I cannot spell 'seize'; I am never sure whether it is an exception to the rule about 'i' before 'e'; I just guess, and fifty times out of a hundred I get it right. On each such occasion we have a counterexample to $CpMp$: it is the case that I am spelling 'seize' correctly but it is not the case that I can spell 'seize' correctly.

Counterexamples similar to these will always be imaginable whenever it is possible to do something by luck rather than by skill. But the distinction between luck and skill is not a marginal matter in this context: it is precisely what we are interested in when our concern is ability, as opposed to logical possibility or opportunity. Of course it is on the basis of people's performances that we attribute skills and abilities to them; but a single performance, however successful, is not normally enough to establish the existence of ability. (I say 'not normally' because a single performance may suffice if the task is sufficiently difficult or complicated to rule out lucky success. Pushing one's wife in a wheelbarrow along a tightrope stretched across Niagara Falls would be a case in point.) But it would only be if a single performance always established an ability that we could offer $CpMp$ as a law of the logic of ability.

This may seem surprising. Surely, if I can either do X or do Y, then either I can do X or I can do Y. For instance, if I can either walk to the door or crawl to the door, then either I can walk to the door or I can crawl to the door. The claim 'I can take it or leave it' is surely a stronger claim than either 'I can take it' or 'I can leave it'. Surely each of the weaker claims severally—let alone their disjunction—can be inferred from the stronger claim.

This is correct, but it does not show that $CMApqAMpMq$ is a logical law if 'M' is interpreted as suggested. In ordinary English 'I can do X or Y' is commonly equivalent to 'I can do X *and* I can do Y', 'I can take it *and* I can leave it'. But if we take 'p' as 'I take it' and 'q' as 'I leave it', then $CMApqAMpMq$ must be read: 'If I can bring it about that either I take it or I leave it, then either I can bring it about that I take it, or I can bring it about that I leave it.' This may perhaps be true, but 'I can bring it about that either I take it or I leave it' is not what is normally meant by 'I can take it or leave it'. If my wife is worried about my smoking, and thinks I have become addicted, I may try to reassure her by saying 'Don't worry about the cigarettes: I can take them or leave them alone.' No doubt the reassurance will be unsuccessful; but it would be downright dishonest if my only grounds for making the statement were my knowledge that, complete addict as I am, I nevertheless make true 'Either I am taking a cigarette or I am leaving cigarettes alone' every time I compulsively reach for the pack.

If we are careful in interpreting $CMApqAMpMq$ we see that it does not express a logical law. Given a pack of cards, I have the ability to pick out on request a card which is either black or red; but I don't have the ability to pick out a red card on request nor the ability to pick out a black card on request. That is to say, the following ($MApq$) is true:

> I can bring it about that either I am picking a red or I am picking a black

but the following ($AMpMq$) is false:

> Either I can bring it about that I am picking a red or I can bring it about that I am picking a black.

Similar counterexamples can be constructed in connection with any other discriminatory skill (e.g. one may have sufficient skill at darts to be quite sure of hitting the board, and yet not be at all sure of obeying either the command 'Hit the top half of the dartboard' or the command 'Hit the bottom half of the dartboard').

The failure of ability to distribute over disjunction is a particularly serious matter for the project of formalization. To see this we must turn briefly from the syntax to the semantics of modal systems.

Kripke and Hintikka and their followers have shown how the semantics of a modal system may be formalized with the aid of the notion of a set of possible worlds and of an alternativeness relation between members of the set. In this type of account the proposition 'Lp' is true in a given possible world if the proposition 'p' is true in every possible world alternative to that possible world; the proposition 'Mp' is true in a given possible world if the proposition 'p' is true in some possible world alternative to that possible world.

The philosophical interest of possible-world semantics is that it enables us to systematize our intuitions about the truth-conditions of propositions containing various modal operators. Formal semantics does not enable us to dispense with intuition: we still have to use our intuitions as rational users of language to decide whether or not a given formal semantics captures the informal meaning of an ordinary language modal word. But we can apply our intuitions not just piecemeal to particular formulae—which may well result in contradictory upshots—but to systems as a whole. In the light of this one is then able to make a rational decision between conflicting intuitions in particular cases.

In effect it is the alternativeness relation on which we have to focus the beam of philosophical intuition. The Kripke-Hintikka approach permits the alternativeness relation to have a wide variety of properties: the two-placed relation of alternativeness may or may not be, for instance, transitive, symmetrical or reflexive. There are necessary relationships between the properties of the alternativeness relation in the semantics and the different syntactic systems: thus a semantic system in which the alternativeness relation is reflexive and also transitive and symmetrical will make true under every interpretation all and only the theses of the Lewis system S5.

In relating the formal modal operators with the modal words of ordinary language, consequently, it is important to direct one's attention to the interpretation of the alternativeness relation. For epistemic logic, for instance, a world $W2$ will be alternative to a world $W1$ if it is a world in which whatever is known in $W1$ is true. A world W_2 will be alternative to W_1 in the logic of opportunity if in W_2 all constraining forces operative in W_1 have achieved their effect.

Now what would be the corresponding intuitive account of the alternativeness relation for a logic of ability? One suggestion which comes to mind is that in the logic of ability W_2 is alternative to W_1 if in W_2 all the abilities present in W_1 have been exercised.[9] At first sight this seems reasonable enough. But reflection shows that there is something wrong with the idea of a world in which all A's abilities are exercised. For suppose that for some ϕ A is able to ϕ and is able to ϕ: John, say, can be a smoker and can also be a non-smoker, i.e. not be a smoker. Then in a world in which all John's abilities are exercised, it will be true both that John is a smoker and that he is not a smoker. And that is not a possible but an impossible world.

It is true that people may have inconsistent beliefs and may be under incompatible obligations: so that a world in which all a person's beliefs were true, and a world in which all his obligations were fulfilled, may be as impossible as a world in which all his abilities are exercised. That is why it has been found convenient in doxastic and deontic logic to adopt the assumption that one is dealing with rational belief and reasonable obligation. This is a justifiable simplification, because it is a defect in beliefs and obligations to be inconsistent: a defect which calls in question *pro tanto* their genuineness as beliefs and obligations. But with ability it is not so. That I have the ability to ϕ in no way weakens the claim that I have the ability not to ϕ: it is a merit, not a defect, in an ability that it is accompanied with an ability of a contrary kind and is therefore an ability which can be exercised at will: indeed it is a mark of volitional ability, as opposed to natural power, that it should be a two-way ability of this kind.

The difficulty in applying possible world semantics to the logic of ability goes further than the problem of finding the appropriate alternativeness relation, however. In the different modal logics some principles follow from special assumptions about the nature of the alternativeness relation while others follow from the basic

---

[9] Analogy with the other cases would suggest that if this were the appropriate relation then the 'can' of ability should be represented as a strong modal operator ('L') not, as we have so far supposed, a weak one like the other 'can's.

framework of possible world semantics. But one of the principles which we earlier gave reason for rejecting—the distribution law, $EAMpMqMApq$—is a principle of this kind. On the usual analysis, the second half of this says that if a disjunction is true in some possible world, then one of the disjuncts must be true in some possible world. This principle will hold no matter how we choose our possible worlds or specify our alternativeness relation.[10] Hence, if we regard possible world semantics as making explicit what is involved in being a possibility, we must say that ability is not any kind of possibility.

Our failure to account for ability as a type of modality might well be taken as confirmation of the familiar view that posits a conditional analysis of personal powers. In this connection there are three questions which remain to be considered. The first is: what is the correct analysis of 'I can if I choose'? The second is, whether the sense of 'I can', where this reports an ability, can be given by a conditional which makes no use of a modal verb of ability. The third is, what are the consequences of our discussion of 'can' for the traditional problem of the relationship between liberty of indifference and liberty of spontaneity?

Ayers, it will be remembered, displayed hostility to the notion of a conditional analysis of personal powers. While discussing another topic, however, he offers a suggestion which seems to me to show the way to a correct solution of the long-standing puzzle about how to analyse expressions such as 'I can if I choose'. He is dealing with the objection that 'the car could do 100 only if there were petrol' seems to suggest, against his theory, that the existence of powers cannot depend on extrinsic factors. Considering the statement 'the lorry could do 70 mph if it were not heavily laden' he says

A lorry that can only do 70mph if it is empty is less powerful than a lorry that can do 70mph even when fully laden. Yet how are we to mark the difference in power between them if it is true to say categorically of them both that they can do the action in question, i.e. can do 70mph. It seems helpful to suggest that we take the if-clause to modify, not the whole main-clause, but simply the description of the action: doing 70-

---

[10] For this important point I am indebted to Professor R. Stalnaker.

heavily-laden and doing 70-without-a-load are different performances, species, so to speak of the genus 'doing 70'. (p. 101)

We can apply this suggestion to the vexed question of the correct
analysis of 'I can if I choose'. Many parties to this inquiry have
assumed that in the expression 'I can if I choose' the 'if' clause
expresses a condition on the ability. They have then gone on to
argue whether it was an ordinary 'if' or a special 'if' analogous to
the 'if' in 'there are biscuits on the table if you want them'.
Davidson has recently argued that in such cases no special 'if' is
called for.[11] Be that as it may, it is a mistake to read 'I can if I
choose' as equivalent to 'If I choose, I can'. 'I can if I choose' is
elliptical for 'I can ϕ if I choose', where the appropriate substitution for 'ϕ' will be given by the context; and in 'I can ϕ if I
choose' the 'if' clause is to be taken with the ϕ, as qualifying the
exercise, not the ability. (Consider the capacity to weep: a child
does not have this capacity at all when new-born; I do; but I
don't have the ability, which an actress would have, to weep-
when-I-choose or weep-if-I-choose. In 'I can weep at will', 'I can
weep to order' the adverbials affect not the 'can' but the 'weep'.)

How rightly to analyse the explicit conditional 'I can if I
choose' is a different question from whether the analysis of the
straightforward 'I can ϕ should yield an implicit conditional.
This was the subject of a famous debate which began in the 1950s
between Professor P. Nowell-Smith and the late J. L. Austin: in
the words of the latter: are cans constitutionally iffy?

The protagonists concentrated much of their attention on the
'all-in' can, the notion of 'can' which is used in 'can do otherwise' in discussions of responsibility, the notion of 'power' which
is used when we talk of what is in our power, a concept which
combines both ability ('personal powers', confusingly, in Ayers'
sense) and opportunity. On one point at issue it seems to me that
Austin was right against Nowell-Smith: even ability plus opportunity plus all-out effort does not guarantee success in the exercise
of a skill. As Austin said in a famous footnote

Consider the case where I miss a very short putt and kick
myself because I could have holed it. It is not that I should
have holed it if I had tried: I did try, and missed. It is not that
I should have holed it if conditions had been different: that

[11] In *Essays on Freedom of Action*, ed. Honderich.

might of course be so but I am talking about conditions as they precisely were, and asserting that I could have holed it. There is the rub. Nor does 'I can hole it this time' mean that I shall hole it this time if I try or anything else: for I may try and miss, and yet not be convinced that I could not have done it; indeed, further experiments may confirm my belief that I could have done it that time although I did not.

But if I tried my hardest, say, and missed, surely there *must* have been *something* that caused me to fail, that made me unable to succeed? So that I *could not* have holed it. Well, a modern belief in science, in there being an explanation of everything, may make us assent to this argument. But such a belief is not in line with the traditional beliefs enshrined in the word *can*: according to *them*, a human ability or power or capacity is inherently liable not to produce success, on occasion, and that for no reason (or are bad luck and bad form sometimes reasons?). (*Philosophical Papers*, 166)

This seems correct. But one must, I think, concede to Nowell Smith that 'I can ϕ' entails: if I have the opportunity to ϕ, and if I do my best to ϕ, then I normally will ϕ. An ability which regularly failed to come off, a skill whose possessor was *always* off form, would not be a genuine ability. ('When I'm on form, I can box better than Muhammad Ali. It's just that I've never yet been on form.') There is this much truth in the conditional analysis of ability. Indeed, as observed, all the difficulties we encountered in analysing ability as a modality may be taken as telling in support of a conditional analysis.

On the other hand critics of the conditional analysis are right that the conditional analysis of ability is not a causal conditional analysis. Ayers is right to reject the position that 'character, or motive or attitude and so on comprises a third variable knowledge of which, together with a knowledge of abilities and circumstances will enable us to predict action'. He is right to reject the position because volition is not a third independently ascertainable variable. All that is involved in a person's wanting to do something may simply be his doing it, his doing it unconstrained.

What are the consequences of all this with respect to the importance of the distinction between liberty of indifference and liberty of spontaneity? In the light of what we have said, it seems obvious that liberty of spontaneity entails the two-way power that is part of liberty of indifference. Something can only be done because it is wanted if it is something that one has an ability not to do. One must have the ability not to ø if one is to ø because one wants to. (One need not necessarily have an opportunity, as Locke showed: a man who stays in a room because he wants to, when unknown to himself it is locked, has the ability but not the opportunity to leave it.) There seems to be truth in the Aristotelian contention that it is only to agents who are of a kind to be able both to do X and not do X that one can attribute wants or desires to do X, as opposed to tendencies to do X. It need not follow from this that when somebody does X this cannot be explained by saying that he wanted to do X, unless it was on that occasion in his power not to do X. For it is only in his power not to do X if he has both ability and *opportunity*. But if an agent does X because he wants to, in circumstances where he has no opportunity not to do X, this can only be because there is some action Y, which would constitute trying not to do X, which he has the opportunity to do. There is thus a necessary relationship between liberty of spontaneity and liberty of indifference, but not the simple one which might have been expected.

The notion of power involved here does not seem to be one which is incompatible with predictability, much less incompatible with determinism. On occasion it may well be true that I can do X even if it is predictable that I will not do X. There is nothing contradictory in saying that I can, but will not, do X any more than there is anything contradictory in saying that I could have done X but did not do X. Thirty seconds ago I did not lift my left leg; but I could have lifted my left leg and my not having done so did not take away the power (the ability and opportunity) that I then had.

As Aristotle saw, liberty of spontaneity applies also to animals; they do things because they want to. But they do so only in so far as they enjoy the two-way power involved in liberty of indifference. It is because the dog can run home that we say he doesn't want to when he disobeys the master's command and pursues the rabbit instead. That is one reason why plants don't have wants; it is because they do not have the capacity to act otherwise. (When a plant does something unexpected, we look for an external cause.)

In human wants of the volitional kind, liberty of spontaneity is linked with liberty of indifference because volition is the rational consideration of an action and as we have seen, rational consideration is ineradicably defeasible.

On the other hand, to the extent that the conditional analysis of human ability is correct, it seems that liberty of indifference must involve liberty of spontaneity. For according to that view the logic of human abilities is intimately connected with such notions as trying, wanting, intending, and choosing. Whatever may turn out to be the most plausible conditional translation of the 'can's of ability, it seems clear that the antecedents must concern mental states or events which constitute volitions or their manifestations. Thus the two-way powers characteristic of rational agents seem *eo ipso* to be powers to act as one wants.

Since Hobbes and Hume, many people have thought that liberty of spontaneity was compatible with determinism. If we are correct in regarding liberty of spontaneity and liberty of indifference as inextricably linked in this way, this can only be the case if liberty of indifference also is compatible with determinism.

VIII

FREEDOM AND
DETERMINISM

'The problems of freewill', said Tolstoy, 'from earliest times has occupied the best intellects of mankind and has from earliest times appeared in all its colossal significance. The problem lies in the fact that if we regard man as a subject for observation from whatever point of view—theological, historical, ethical or philosophic—we find the universal law of necessity to which he (like everything else that exists) is subject. But looking upon man from within ourselves—man as the object of our own inner consciousness of self—we feel ourselves to be free.' The existence of freedom, Tolstoy thought, was incompatible with the existence of scientific laws. Reason teaches us the laws of necessity: the consciousness of freedom must at best be the expression of ignorance of laws. 'It is necessary'—these are the last words of *War and Peace*—'to renounce a freedom that does not exist and to recognise a dependence of which we are not personally conscious.'

Like Tolstoy, Dr. Johnson regarded freedom and determinism as incompatible; because of the incompatibility, he rejected determinism. 'We know our will is free and there is an end on it,' he said. Tolstoy and Johnson present, in effect, two parallel and conflicting arguments.

1 Freedom and determinism are incompatible
   We know determinism is true
   Therefore, freedom is illusory
2 Freedom and determinism are incompatible
   We know we are free
   Therefore, determinism is false

Many distinguished philosophers have considered the possibility of rejecting the major premiss which is common to both Johnson and Tolstoy.

Philosophers who have rejected the incompatibility of freedom and determinism have commonly made a distinction between various senses of freedom. They have admitted that there are senses in which freedom is incompatible with determinism but have denied that we know that we are in these senses free. The sense in which we know we are free, they have claimed, is one in which freedom leaves room for determinism.

The distinction between liberty of indifference and liberty of spontaneity was a distinction of this kind. Once the distinction had been drawn it seemed easy enough for the defender of determinism to reply to Dr. Johnson's argument. 'The freedom which is incompatible with determinism', he could say, 'is liberty of indifference; the freedom which we know we have is liberty of spontaneity. Whether or not we enjoy liberty of indifference cannot be a matter of bluff common-sense experience. For how could experience show us that there is no sufficient antecedent condition for our actions? Whether there are such conditions depends on the nature of the totality of physical laws governing life in our universe; and how could the introspection even of a Dr. Johnson be sufficient to establish the nature of these? How could one feel within oneself the lack of a law correlating one's present action with one's previous history? "All theory", Dr. Johnson said, in another pronouncement, "is against the freedom of the will; all experience for it." What theory was against was liberty of indifference, what experience was for was liberty of spontaneity.'

But if liberty of spontaneity and liberty of indifference cannot be possessed without each other, as we argued at the end of the last chapter, we cannot so easily decide whether free will and determinism are compatible with each other. The theory that they are—the theory of 'compatibilism'—will only be defensible if liberty of indifference, no less than liberty of spontaneity, can be reconciled with determinism.

Thomas Hobbes, in *Leviathan*, said: 'Liberty and Necessity are Consistent: as in the water, that hath not only liberty, but a necessity of descending by the Channel; so likewise in the Actions which men voluntarily do; which, because they proceed from their will, proceed from liberty; and yet, because every act of man's will, and every desire and inclination proceedeth from some cause, and that from another cause, in a continuall chaine, whose first link in the hand of God the first of all causes, proceed from necessity' (chapter 21).

'This is a brutish liberty', objected his adversary, Bishop Bramhall, 'such a liberty as a bird hath to fly when her wings are clipped. Is not this a ridiculous liberty? Lastly (which is worse than all these) such a liberty as a river hath to descend down the channel. Such is T.H.'s liberty.'

'I did let him know,' Hobbes replied, 'that a man was free, in those things that were in his power, to follow his will; but that he was not free to will, that is, that his will did not follow his will. Which I expressed in these words: "The question is whether the will to write, or the will to forbear, come upon a man according to his will, or according to any thing else in his own power." He that cannot understand the difference between *free to do it if he will*, and *free to will*, is not fit, as I have said in the stating of the question, to hear this controversy disputed, much less to be a writer in it.'[1]

The compatibilist theory as presented by an author like Hobbes suffers from two principal defects. First, as Bramhall pointed out, it does not do justice to the obvious differences between the modes of action of inanimate agents and of rational agents like human beings. Secondly, it involves an uncritical conception of mental causation. The determinism which is put forward as compatible with liberty is a psychological determinism. It is observed that the fact that we can do what we want does not mean that we can want what we want: we may be free to do what we will, and yet not free to will what we will. For reasons given in chapter six, few philosophers would nowadays talk of wants, in quite this unselfconscious manner, as mental events which determine action.

Hobbes' contemporary Arminian opponents, however, themselves spoke in a similarly naïve way about wants as causes of action, as acts of choice being the objects of other acts of choice. This laid them open to a version of the regress argument which we discussed in the early chapters of this book. It is thus stated, in polemic against the Arminians, by the Calvinist theologian Jonathan Edwards in his *Freedom of the Will*.

The meaning [of the Arminians] must be that a man has power

---

[1] *The Questions Concerning Liberty, Necessity and Chance.*

to will as he pleases or chooses to will: that is, he has power by one act of choice, to choose another; by an antecedent act of will to choose a consequent act; and therein to execute his own choice. And if this be their meaning, it is nothing but shuffling with those they dispute with, and baffling their own reason. For still the question returns, wherein lies man's liberty in that antecedent act of will which chose the consequent act? The answer according to the same principles must be, that his liberty in this also lies in his willing as he would, or as he chose, or agreeable to another act of choice preceding that. And so the question returns in infinitum, and the like answer must be made in infinitum: in order to support their opinion there must be no beginning, but free acts of will must have been chosen by foregoing free acts of will, in the soul of every man, without beginning; and so before he had a being, from all eternity. (II, 5)

To regard the mind as a field of paramechanical causes or agents in this way is to enter a maze of blind alleys, and once one is in the maze it matters little whether one takes the determinist or the libertarian turning. Any viable form of compatibilism must do justice to the difference between reasons and causes. If the compatibilist is right to say that A's doing X because he wants to is compatible with the causal predetermination of the event which is his doing X, this will not be because his wanting to do X is a cause that is itself causally determined, but rather because the types of causal determinism that are ruled out by saying that he acted voluntarily do not necessarily exhaust the types of causal determinism that there are.

Pre-eminent among the types of causal determinism that *are* ruled out are psychological determinisms, determinisms in virtue of laws in the statement of which mental predicates must occur non-vacuously. Among determinisms so defined, there are obviously included economic and sociological determinisms. According to the sophisticated compatibilist, however, physiological determinism is on a different footing. There is no incompatibility, he claims, between explanation by neurophysiological states and explanation in terms of wants and intentions; and this is so even if the laws of neurophysiology should turn out in the end to be fundamentally deterministic.

In order to defend this view, most contemporary compatibilists invoke a difference between levels of explanation. The compatibilism of Hobbes and Hume does not involve any differentiation of levels: the level at which the determinism operates is the same as the level at which freedom is experienced, namely that of introspectionist psychology. The post-Kantian compatibilist, instead of distinguishing between liberty of spontaneity and liberty of indifference, replies to Dr. Johnson's modern counterpart by introducing a distinction between levels of description and explanation. He can agree that freedom and indeterminism are incompatible at a single level, while denying that there need be any incompatibility at a different level. He can agree that we know that at the psychological level we are free and therefore at the psychological level undetermined. But he can deny that we know anything about determinism at the physiological level.

The relevance of this to the issue between free will and determinism is as follows. The concepts and vocabulary of physiology are totally different from those employed in the everyday description of human behaviour. It is only actions described in terms of human behaviour that libertarians claim to be free. Even one hundred per cent certain predictability at the level of physiology need not by itself involve any increase in predictability at the human level. For physiological laws will enable us to predict only physiological effects from physiological causes; and we shall need in addition at least translation-rules from the language of physiology into the language of human behaviour. On the other hand, from an action described in human terms a further action described in the same terms may well be predicted; as in certain circumstances from the making of an appointment one may predict the keeping of the appointment. But it would be impossible for prediction in these terms to achieve one hundred per cent certainty, since the everyday language of intention and motive, praise and blame, reward and reprimand presupposes a structure of freedom and limited unpredictability.

This sort of freedom, it seems, is possible without the violation of any physiological laws; just as it is possible to say that a given sequence of coin-tossings is a random sequence without claiming that the laws of motion were suspended for any particular toss. However, it does not seem to be compatible with the existence of sociological or economic laws, since the expression of any such laws would have to make reference to precisely such features of intention and motive as presuppose the structure of freedom and limited unpredictability.

Physiology, however, is in a different position and the crucial question raised by the argument so far is whether there can be translation rules between the language of physiology and the language of human behaviour. If there can, then it seems that human behaviour is as predictable as any physiological event; and physiological determinism will be incompatible with human freedom.

The mere fact that there is no one-one correlation between human actions and physiological events does not settle the question in favour of compatibilism. The problem of overlap occurs between natural languages too (one French word may correspond to many English words, and one English word to many French words) and yet translation is not impossible. And surely, if every movement of a man's hands, every twitch of every muscle was predictable; then surely his whole observable life would be predictable, no matter in what terms it was described? The untidy nature of the translation from physiological into intentional terms does not really count against this. The situation might be compared to a jigsaw puzzle. A man's life, told in the terms which would appear in his biography, might be compared with the picture on the completed puzzle; the physiological events which make up his life might be compared to the pieces of the puzzle. There is no systematic correlation between pieces of the puzzle and details of the picture, neither one-one, many-one, nor one-many. For all that, once the pieces are fitted together, there you have the picture; and anyone who knows how to put the pieces together can *eo ipso* lay down the picture.[2]

The picture is a powerful one: but it is misleading. To see how, we must go back to the definition of liberty of indifference, of the all-in 'can' constituted by ability and opportunity. According to that definition an agent ϕs freely at t if at t he has the ability and the opportunity both to ϕ and not to ϕ. In other words, given that A ϕd at t, in order to show he enjoyed liberty of indifference we have to show four things

---

[2] The argument of the preceding paragraphs is developed at greater length in my paper 'Freedom, Spontaneity and Indifference' on which the present chapter is partly based.

1 A has at t the ability to ϕ
2 A had at t the ability not to ϕ
3 A had at t the opportunity to ϕ at t
4 A had at t the opportunity not to ϕ at t.

The statements of the opportunities, but not of the abilities, have the double temporal qualification discussed in the preceding chapter. Now, on the supposition that free will and physiological determinism are compatible, it will be true both (a) that A ϕd at t because he wanted to ϕ at t; (b) that the physical movements which constituted A's ϕing at t were in accordance with a deterministic physiological law: that is to say, they fell under a physiological description such that there existed a law from which, with a description of the antecedent physiological and physical conditions, it could be deduced that an event of that description would occur.

Now do these suppositions lead to any contradiction? In the light of what we have said about ability, opportunity, and wanting, it seems that they do not. First, whether at t A has the ability to ϕ, and the ability not to ϕ—the two-way power of ϕing—is something which can be settled independently of the circumstances obtaining at t. Provided that A has in the past, and continues in the future, to satisfy the criteria for possessing this ability, 'A can ϕ' will be true of him at this present moment t. Indeed, as Ayers has shown, 'A can ϕ' may be true and yet it be certain that A never will ϕ (perhaps because he will never have an opportunity to ϕ, perhaps because he will never want to ϕ).

What of the factor of opportunity? Clearly, proposition (3) above presents no difficulty: if A does ϕ then he has the opportunity to ϕ: in the logic of opportunity the inference *ab esse ad posse* holds. The crucial question is whether he has the opportunity not to ϕ. Here, the answer is: yes, if—as in this case—the reason that he is not-ϕing is that he wants to ϕ.[3] For, as we said earlier, an opportunity is not removed simply by the presence of a contrary want. But how can it be true that he is ϕing because he wants to if—as may well be the case—the antecedent physiological conditions were such that no event answering to the

[3] The 'if' here cannot be replaced by an 'iff' if Austin is right about putting.

description predictable from them could also be describable as 'not ϕing?' Suppose, e.g., that 'ϕ' is opening one's mouth, and that the physiological prediction is that the lips will be one inch apart: if that is what the physiological description is, how can there be a question of having the opportunity not to open one's mouth at t? Again the answer is: if one of the features on which the physiological prediction is based is a factor which would not have obtained unless the agent had *wanted* to open his mouth, then the physiological prediction does not remove opportunity, and thus does not negative freedom.

But does not this solution boil down to the old compatibilist theory according to which the determinism compatible with freedom is a psychological determinism? No: that would be so only if there were a law-like correlation between wants to open one's mouth, and physiological factors of the kind present in this case. But there need not be any such correlation: indeed we have argued in an earlier chapter that there cannot be. It is perfectly possible for there to be a physiological feature which *in the circumstances of this case* would not be present unless the particular want was present, without there being a general law linking physical and psychological features of the respective kinds. One does not have to look far for an instance of this even where simple physical causation is in question. If I am in a room with a two-way switch, it may be that *as things are* I can put the light on if and only if I put the switch at my end of the corridor down; but there is no uniform connection with this switch's being done and the light's being on; it depends what people have been doing at the other end of the corridor.

It seems, then, that there is no clear reason for thinking compatibilism false. It has not been show that 'I can ϕ at t' (where the 'can' is the all-in 'can') entails that my ϕing, or, as the case may be, my not ϕing, at t is contingent, in the overall sense that it falls under no covering law and has no antecedent sufficient conditions.

This conclusion can be confirmed by an examination of some recent discussions of compatibilism. Professor Anscombe argues thus for incompatibilism.

> My actions are mostly physical movements; if these physical movements are physically predetermined by processes which I

do not control, then my freedom is illusory. The truth of physical indeterminism is then indispensable if we are to make anything of the claim to freedom. (*Causation and Determination*, 26)

I have argued in print that this reasoning depends on Leibniz's law that if x is identical with y then whatever is true of x is also true of y. I took the argument to be to the effect that if my actions are identical with certain physical movements, and if these physical movements are determined, then my actions must be determined. This was unfair to Professor Anscombe, who has often rejected Leibniz's law, stressing, for instance, that an action may be intentional under one description but not under another.[4] None the less, her argument still seems to me invalid.

Does physical determinism entail that the movements constituting my actions are determined by processes I do not control? The answer seems to be that if a universal determinism is true, then at least *some* of the processes determining my movements are outside my control—those for instance which took place before my birth. But it does not follow that *all* the processes determining my movements are outside my control: for it may be that the later stages of the determining process are stages which are within my control; that is to say, they are events and processes constituting actions of the right kind to be exercises of my powers; events and processes which, if I had wished otherwise, would have been other than they in fact are.

But surely, it may be objected, if a certain state of the universe S_1 determines a later state S_2, such that S_1 is quite outside my control (e.g. because it is a state of the universe before my existence began), then S_2 must also be quite outside my control![5] No: for part of what is determined by S_1 may be that S_2 will have been brought about by factors within my control. There is no more reason to accept the objection than to accept the argument that if some named human beings are descendants of people who are no descendants of mine, then those named human beings are no descendants of mine. My grandchildren can surely be

[4] Moreover, some of the arguments I used against Leibniz's law ('Freedom, Spontaneity and Indifference', 97 f.) now seem to me rather dubious.

[5] For this formulation of the objection I am indebted to Professor B. A. O. Williams.

descendants of mine even though they are descendants of my grandparents who were no descendants of mine.

Professor Wiggins, in a sympathetic presentation of the incompatibilist position, presents the following argument.

Suppose that R records the movement of extending a finger, and A says that the person in question kept still. Suppose that we have a law of nature that

(1) It is inevitable at t' that (if C at t then R at t')

Given the explanation of 'R' and 'A' we have

(2) It is inevitable at t' that (if R at t' then not A at t')

Then if this sort of inevitability is transitive we have

(3) It is inevitable at t' (if C at t then not A at t')

Can we then say that the man could have kept still even though at the earlier moment t, C obtained? Wiggins replies:

Suppose that it is asserted that, in spite of the fact that (1), (2), (3) obtained, and in spite of the fact C, and in spite of the fact that the man made the movement and extended his finger (R was true) and did not keep still (Not-A was true).

(4) he could have kept still at t'

I am not sure how to analyse 'he could have kept still at t'' in terms of possibility or necessity, but it seems plain that (4) must at least entail that it was not physically or historically impossible at t' that the man should keep still at t'. For surely

(5) X can ø at t only if it is not necessary at t that not (ø at t')

He who maintains (4) must by (5) admit

(6) It is possible at t' (A at t')

But, Wiggins goes on, by uncontroversial modal principles we can now get

(7) It is possible at t' (not C at t)

But how could it be historically possible at t' for not C at t'? t' is later than t. By t' there is nothing anybody or anything can do about C. But, then, if (1) and (2) are true—as determinism demands—the fault can only lie in (4).[6]

After what we have seen in the earlier part of this chapter, it will be obvious that Wiggins' principle numbered (5) above

---

[6] 'Towards a Reasonable Libertarianism'.

simply begs the whole question against the incompatibilist. It *assumes* that the modality involved in talking of physical impossibility is the same as that involved in talking of human ability and opportunity. But that is the whole question at issue. This is perhaps obscured from him by his use of the notion of 'historical inevitability' which may perhaps be a hybrid of the two modalities. He writes:

> By 'it is historically inevitable at time t' that p' is intended something like this—whatever anybody or anything does at t' or thereafter it can make no difference to p, p being either a law of logic or a law of nature or already history, or being the logical or physical consequence of what is already history. This definition already includes the notion of possibility, but this is no objection. (p. 45)

He cannot really mean 'whatever anybody does after t can make no difference'—it would make a difference, for instance, if someone brought it about that not p. What he must mean is surely 'whatever anybody or anything *can* do at t' or thereafter can make no difference'. And now the definition includes two different 'can's; and so it suffers not merely from a harmless circularity, but from a question-begging ambiguity.

This much must be conceded to the incompatibilist, however. Suppose that it is physiologically determined that I will not ϕ, in the sense that it is physiologically determined that no physical movements will take place which will be describable as my ϕing. In that case, then there will be many descriptions ψ of what ϕing would, in the circumstances amount to, such that I can ψ would be false. For instance, in the circumstances described, for me to ϕ would *ex hypothesi* be for me to violate some law of nature. But clearly it is not, ever, in my power to violate a law of nature.

This consideration does not establish incompatibilism, however, unless we argue that if I cannot violate a law of nature, then I cannot move my little finger. And this argument would be incorrect. For there is something wrong with the pattern of argument

I can (cannot) do X
Doing X is doing Y
Therefore I can (cannot) do Y.

The principle
If to ϕ is to ψ, and I can ϕ, then I can ψ

which seems harmless enough is in fact false, if it is considered as having unrestrictedly general application.

There are many cases where I can ϕ but will not. In such cases, there will be descriptions ψ of ϕing which will describe it in terms of the fact that I am in fact, not going to ϕ. Thus, let us suppose that I am going to eat my cake. I can, if I want, have my cake, but I am not going to have my cake, I am going to eat it. Given the facts of the case, to have my cake would be to have it and eat it too. But I can, if I want, have it. So, if the principle is valid, I can have my cake and eat it too.

The argument pattern set out above works, of course, if the identity between doing X and doing Y is a logically necessary one; but it does not work if what is meant by the second premiss is simply that a particular instance of doing X is the same as a particular instance of doing Y, i.e. that a particular exercise of the ability to do X falls also under the description 'doing Y'. I may be able to hit the dartboard; on a particular occasion I may hit the dartboard by hitting the centre of the bull, but it by no means follows that I am capable of hitting the centre of the bull. Any particular exercise of power and skill will have other descriptions besides the one which occurs in the specification of the power; and the possession of the power specified in no way involves the possession of the power to perform acts answering to those other descriptions.

Some who have considered the argument form laid out above regard it as containing an equivocation: in the 'do X' in the first premiss and the conclusion, they say, the 'X' has to be replaced by a generic act, a description of an act-type; whereas in the second premiss 'doing X' refers to a particular act, an act-token. This seems to be basically the same objection as my own, stated in a different terminology. The breakdown of the principle to which, it seems, the compatibilist must appeal occurs in either case. And it occurs for the same reason, namely, because of the principle that there is no individuation without actualization.[7]

---

[7] So far as I know the first philosopher to point out the fallaciousness of this pattern of argument was Duns Scotus, discussing the problem of divine foreknowledge. He puts to himself the following objection.

Quia sequitur Deus novit me sessurum cras, et non sedebo cras, ergo

Notice that the argument makes no appeal to a difference of levels between the two descriptions of the act performed; indeed in the example just given both descriptions were at an everyday level of common language. But obviously the same types of consideration apply also in those cases where there is a crossing of levels. The difficulty of giving illuminating examples here is that once one alters the level of description, then what is the agent at one level becomes an inappropriate subject for the attribution of powers at the other level. When we want to consider the validity of the argument that if the molecules composing my mouth can move only in one way then I cannot say anything other than I do, we have to consider a conclusion which differs from the premiss not only in its predicate but also in its subject. This is not of course an unimportant point, nor one irrelevant to the whole issue we have been discussing. But if the argument does not hold in the case where it would be most likely to hold, namely where the subject of the verb in the conclusion is the same as the subject of the verb in the predicate, and where both verbs belong to the same vocabulary, there seems little reason to believe that the argument will work elsewhere.

I have been arguing that it is unproven that determinism and freedom are incompatible. I should make clear in conclusion that my motive in doing so has not been a belief that determinism is true. I have merely been criticizing one argument purporting to show it to be false.

Whether determinism is true or false seems to me something which cannot be settled on *a priori* grounds, if it can ever be

Deus decipitur; igitur a simili sequitur Deus novit me sessurum, et possum non sedere cras, ergo Deus potest decipi. Prima est manifesta, quia credens illud quo non est in re, decipitur. probo—ex hoc quod consequentia teneat quia sicut ad duas de inesse sequitur conclusio de inesse, ita ex una de inesse et altera de possibili sequitur conclusio de possibili. (*Ordinatio*, in dist. XVI, 39 q 1a)

Scotus' solution is to deny that a modalized conclusion such as 'I can bring it about that God is mistaken' follows from 'I can bring it about that I sit tomorrow' and 'If I sit tomorrow then God is mistaken'. It isn't, he says, true that *ex una de inesse et altera de possibili sequitur conclusio de possibili*. His counterexample is: *possum ferre istud pondus in a, et possum ferre illud pondus in a, igitur possum simul ferre hoc et illum in a*. That is: suppose I am carrying my own suitcase, A. In these circumstances, to carry my wife's suitcase B, would be to carry both A and B. But though I can carry A, I can't carry both A and B.

settled at all. If the argument of the present chapter has had any
validity, there is no clear argument from the existence of free
will to indeterminism. Nor is there any valid argument to the
effect that indeterminism is presupposed as a condition of the significance of ordinary language and of the rationality of human
social institutions. Unless there is indeterminism, it is argued, then
we have all been talking nonsense for much of our lives. The argument fails. It is true that when, in ordinary life, we ask whether
an agent could have done otherwise—for instance, when we are
wondering whether to hold him responsible, and punish him for
some misdeed—we are using the language of indifference. But, as
we have been at pains to argue, liberty of indifference does not
demand determinism. And even if it did, it might well be that we
can make the distinctions we make, and serve the purposes we
have in making these distinctions, without accepting the theoretical account on which they are putatively based. We could
continue to accept the same criteria for the appropriateness of the
attribution of responsibility, while denying that they were criteria
for the absence of sufficient antecedent conditions. The distinctions now made between determined and free actions would
reappear as distinctions between different patterns of causation of
actions.

Ever since the time of Aristotle men have been found to argue
that if determinism is true, then all effort is a waste of time. The
argument was succinctly put, in the context of theological determinism, by John Milton (in his anti-Calvinist *de doctrina
Christiana*)

> If God has made an absolute decree of salvation for me, then
> whatever I do in the contrary sense I will not perish. 'But he
> has also decreed a good life as the means of salvation.' Well
> then, if God has decreed it I cannot help sooner or later leading
> a good life; meanwhile I will do whatever I like. If I never lead
> a good life, I will discover that I was never destined for salva-
> tion, and whatever good deeds I may have done would have
> been a waste of effort.

The principle 'If it is determined that I will be saved, then no
matter what I do I will be saved' is ambiguous. Since the truth-
functional 'if p then q' is true whenever q is true, then if 'I will be
saved' is true, both

If I live a good life I will be saved

and

If I live a bad life, I will be saved

are true. It is in this sense that it is true that if it is determined I will be saved, then no matter what I do I will be saved: i.e. 'If *p* I will be saved' is true no matter what is substituted for the antecedent.

But neither of the truth-functional conditionals are of any help when one is trying to plan what to do *in order to be* saved. What is needed is a conditional of a non-truth functional kind, sufficient to ground such counterfactuals as

If I led a bad life, I would be saved.

And the principle stated above is not necessarily true if interpreted in the sense 'If it is determined that I will be saved then no matter what I might do I would be saved.' The point made here about the theological case is of general validity against arguments to show that determinism makes all effort wasted.

It is sometimes argued that the existence of chance events shows the existence of indeterminism at a macroscopic level. Thus Geach writes

> The theory of probability arose, Voltaire tells us, from a problem posed by an *homme du monde* to an *austère Janséniste*. The Chevalier de Meré, a seasoned gambler, had observed that there is a slightly worse than even chance of getting a double six in twentyfour throws of a pair of dice, but a slightly better than even chance of getting a six in four throws of a single dice. Pascal's calculations, based on assumptions about equal possibilities, exactly agreed with this experience. Again, being kicked to death by a horse is just what people would count as a matter of luck, bad luck of course: and during the lifetime of the Hohenzollern Empire German cavalrymen perished in this way strictly in accordance with the laws of probability ... There is massive evidence, then, that classes of events that would naively be counted as chance events really do conform to an *a priori* standard of contingency in which now this, now that, possible alternative is realised. (*God and the Soul*, 95–6)

But surely this only shows that it is possible to give paired descriptions of particular events such that there is only a random correlation between the two descriptions of each pair: it does not show that such events fall under *no* description such that an event falling under that description could not have been infallibly predicted. Thus, the cases in point show that if an event falls under the description 'Fall of a true die' or under the description 'death by horsekick of a cavalryman of the *n*th German regiment' it will be a matter of pure chance, as determined by the *a priori* calculus of probabilities, whether it falls under the descriptions 'fall with the six uppermost' or 'death occurring in the year *m*'. But it does not show anything, one way or the other, about the possibility of giving descriptions of the events in question which could have been determined in advance by the laws of Newtonian mechanics or equine physiology.

The arguments in favour of determinism are in no better case. It is indeed difficult to account for the popularity of determinism in philosophical circles, given its unfashionableness in physics. No one, I think, suggests that determinism might be a datum of experience or introspection as some have suggested that freedom might be. The main sources of belief in determinism among philosophers seem to be a philosophical confusion and an extrapolation from the history of science.

In the passage from Tolstoy from which I started there can be detected a confusion between the notion of a set of laws being *exceptionless* and its being *complete*. 'If one man only out of millions once in a thousand years had the power of acting freely, i.e. as he chose, it is obvious that one single free act of that man in violation of the laws would be enough to prove that laws governing all human action cannot possibly exist.' Tolstoy thinks that an action must be either determined by laws or be a violation of laws. But laws may be exceptionless (apply to all items of a certain kind) without being complete in the sense of determining each item of that kind: as the laws of chess are exceptionless (they apply to every move in the game) without determining every move in the game (as the rules of, e.g., beggar-my-neighbour do, so that every move can be predicted from the initial hands dealt). Philosophers more professional than Tolstoy have not escaped this confusion.

Others seem to have based their determinism on a certain view of the history of the progress of science. All the natural sciences, we may be told, have made progress to the extent that they have sought sufficient antecedent conditions for phenomena and have refused to be content with the suggestion that different phenomena might arise in identical antecedent conditions. Does it not therefore seem reasonable to suppose that the way to success for the sciences of human behaviour must also lie in the uncovering of the determinants of the phenomena which constitute such behaviour?

In answer to this one may query whether we have any reason to believe that there can be a successful science of human behaviour; but this response will no doubt appear unhelpful and pessimistic. It may be more productive to inquire from what features of the history of scientific progress one is supposed to extrapolate. Is one to point to the success of deterministic explanation in Newtonian mechanics, or to its lack of success in stimulus-response psychology? It is impossible not to be impressed by the present availability of mechanistic explanations for many physical phenomena which were explained teleologically until the time of Descartes. But perhaps one should be no less impressed by the continuing impossibility of explaining, in terms of sufficient antecedent conditions, any psychological phenomenon which would have been regarded as voluntary in the time of Aristotle.

BIBLIOGRAPHY

ANSCOMBE, G. E. M., *Intention*, Oxford, 1957.
—— 'Thought and Action in Aristotle' in *New Essays on Plato and Aristotle*, ed. R. Bambrough, London, 1965.
—— *Causality and Determination*, Cambridge, 1971.
AQUINAS, ST. THOMAS, *Summa Theologica*.
—— *De Veritate*.
ARISTOTLE, *Prior Analytics*.
—— *De Motu Animalium*.
—— *Nicomachean Ethics*.
—— *Eudemian Ethics*.
—— *Metaphysics*.
ARMSTRONG, D. M., *Belief, Truth, and Knowledge*, Cambridge, 1972.
AUNE, B., 'Can' in *The Encyclopedia of Philosophy*, New York, 1967.
AUSTIN, J. L., *Philosophical Papers*, Oxford, 1961.
AYERS, M., *The Refutation of Determinism*, London, 1968.
BELL, D., 'Imperatives and the Will', *Proceedings of the Aristotelian Society*, 1965–6, 129 ff.
BENNETT, J., *Rationality*, London, 1964.
BENTHAM, J., *Principles of Morals and Legislation*.
BRAMHALL, see HOBBES.
CASTANEDA, H.-N., 'Imperatives, Decisions and "Oughts"' in *Morality and the Language of Conduct*, Detroit, 1965.
CHOMSKY, N., *Syntactic Structures*, The Hague, 1964.
DAVIDSON, D., 'How is Weakness of the Will possible?' in *Moral Concepts*, ed. Feinberg, Oxford, 1969.
—— 'Mental Events' in *Experience and Theory*, ed. Foster and Swanson, London, 1970.
—— 'Agency' in *Agent, Action and Reason*, ed. Binkley, Bronaugh and Marras, Toronto.

—— 'Freedom to Act' in *Essays on Freedom of Action*, ed. Honderich, London, 1973.

DESCARTES, R., *Les Passions de l'Ame*.

DUMMETT, M., 'Truth', *Proceedings of the Aristotelian Society*, 1958–9, pp. 141 ff.

DUNS SCOTUS, *Ordinatio* (Vatican City, 1950–   ).

EDWARDS, J., *Freedom of the Will*, Yale, 1957.

FRANKFURT, H., 'Freedom of the Will and the Concept of a Person', *Journal of Phil.*, 1971, 5 ff.

FREGE, G., *Philosophical Writings*, ed. Geach and Black, Oxford, 1952.

FREUD, S., *The Standard Edition of the Complete Psychological Works*, London, 1953–64.

GEACH, P. T., *Mental Acts*, London, 1957.

—— 'The Will', *Newman Philosophy of Science Bulletin*, January 1958, July 1958.

—— 'Aquinas' in *Three Philosophers*, Oxford, 1961.

—— *God and the Soul*, London, 1969.

—— 'Kenny on Practical Reasoning' in *Logic Matters*, Oxford, 1972.

GIBBS, B., 'Real Possibility', *American Philosophical Quarterly*, 1970.

HARE, R. M., *The Language of Morals*, Oxford, 1952.

—— *Freedom and Reason*, Oxford, 1963.

—— *Practical Inferences*, London, 1971.

HOBBES, T., *Leviathan*.

—— (with BRAMHALL), *The Questions concerning Liberty, Necessity and Chance* in volume V of the English Works, ed. Molesworth, London, 1841.

HOFSTADTER and McKINSEY, 'The Logic of Imperatives', *Philosophy of Science*, 1939, 446 ff.

HONORÉ, A. M., 'Can and Can't', *Mind*, 1964.

HUME, D., *A Treatise of Human Nature*.

JAMES, W., *Principles of Psychology* (Dover edn.), London and New York, 1950.

KENNY, A., *Action, Emotion and Will*, London, 1963.

—— 'Intention and Purpose' in *Journal of Philosophy*, 1966; revised version in Summers, *Essays in Legal Philosophy*, 1968.

—— 'Practical Inference', *Analysis* supplement, 1966.

—— 'Freedom, Spontaneity and Indifference' in *Essays on Freedom of Action*, ed. Honderich, London, 1973.

—— *The Anatomy of the Soul*, Oxford, 1974.

—— (with Longuet-Higgins and others), *The Origin of Mind* (Gifford Lectures, 1972–3), Edinburgh, 1974.

—— 'The Logic of Ability', *Acta Philosophica Fennica*, Helsinki, forthcoming.

—— 'Aquinas on the Will', in *Proceedings of the Aquinas Centenary Celebrations in Calgary*, forthcoming.

Locke, D., 'Reasons, Wants and Causes', *American Philosophical Quarterly*, 1975.

Mill, J. S., *System of Logic*, Book III, ch. X.

Milton, J., *De Doctrina Christiana*.

Nowell-Smith, P., 'Ifs and Cans', *Theoria*, 1960.

Palmer, F., *A Linguistic Study of the English Verb*, London, 1965.

Pears, D., *Predicting and Deciding*, Oxford, 1965.

—— Comments on 'Wanting: Some Pitfalls' (see Hare), in *Agent, Action and Reason*, ed. Binkley *et al.*

—— 'Rational Explanation of Actions and Psychological Determinism' in *Essays on Freedom of Action*, ed. Honderich, London, 1973.

Russell, B., 'The Philosophy of Logical Atomism' in *Logic and Knowledge*, London, 1956.

Ryle, G., *The Concept of Mind*, London, 1948.

Snyder, D. P., *Modal Logic and its Applications*, New York, 1971.

Stenius, E., *Wittgenstein's Tractatus*, Oxford, 1960.

Taylor, C., *The Explanation of Behaviour*, London, 1964.

von Wright, G. H., *An Essay on Modal Logic*, Amsterdam, 1951.

—— *Norm and Action*, London, 1963.

—— 'On So-called Practical Inference', *Acta Sociologica*, 1972.

Wiggins, D., 'Towards a reasonable libertarianism', in *Essays on Freedom of Action*, ed. Honderich, London, 1973.

Wittgenstein, L., *Tractatus Logico-Philosophicus*, London, 1922.

—— *The Blue and Brown Books*, Oxford, 1958.

—— *Philosophical Investigations*, Oxford, 1953.

INDEX

A priori knowledge, 42
Ability, 2, 105ff, 123–44, 151, 154–5
Act *v.* activity, 54
Action, Emotion and Will, 27–35, 54, 75
Activity *v.* performance, 54
Actors on stage (example), 36 f
Actualization, primary *v.* secondary, 123
Actus (= actualization), 24
Actus elicitus ('elicited act'), 23 ff, 35
Actus imperatus ('commanded act'), 23 ff, 27
Affirming the consequent, 70
Agency, 46 f, 55
Akolasia (intemperance), 17
Akrasia (weakness of will), 14, 18, 47, 102–7, 114 f
Alarm clock (example), 33
Alethic modality, 130 f
All-in 'can', 131, 141
Alternativeness, 138
Andersen fairy tale (example), 11
Anger, 115
Animals, 2, 5, 15, 18 ff, 46 f, 48 f, 51, 143
Anomalousness of mental, 121
Anscombe, G. E. M., 18, 37, 48, 51, 152
Anthropomorphism, 51
Antony and Cleopatra (example), 17
Appetition, 16, 70–96
Aquinas, St. Thomas, 11, 19–28, 47, 49, 93–5
Arche (originating cause) of action, 15 f

Aristotle, 7, 15 f, 25, 49, 71 ff, 83, 88, 94 f, 97 f, 108, 114, 115
Armstrong, D., 51
Assent, 90
Assertion, 30, 36
Assertion-sign, 35 ff
Assertoric sentences and logic, 74, 86 f
Attempt, 60
Augustine, St., 41
Austin, J. L., 18, 131, 151
Autonomy, 3
Ayers, M. R., 124 f, 131, 140

Backsliding, see akrasia
Balloon (example), 111
Beggar-my-neighbour (example), 110
Beliefs, 29, 34, 48, 108–18
Bell, D. R., 31–5
Bentham, J., 59
Best, acting for, 102
Betting, 75
Bicycle (example), 52
Bogey, Col. (example), 92
Bone, scratching for (example), 20
Boulesis (wish), 16
Bouleusis (deliberation), 16
Brain, 7
Bramhall, Bishop, 147
Breathing (example) 22, 53
Buridan's Ass, 102

Cairns, L. J., 60
Cake, having and eating (example), 156 f
'Can', 123–44

Capacities, 2, 4, 9 f
Car (example), 31, 125–7
Cards, pack of (example) 137
Castaneda, H-N., 76
Cat on mat, seeing v. willing, 42
Causes v. reasons, 107–9
Cavalry, Hohenzollern (example), 160
Chain of causes, 146
Chain of command, 91
Change of mind, 32
Character, 16 f
Cheshire Cat, 9
China (example), 84, 92
Choice, 16, 18
Climber and rope (example), 114, 121, 134
Cloak syllogism, 72, 83, 88, 97
Coffee, smell of (example), 117
Cognitive v. affective, 42
Coleridge, L. J., 61
Commands, 30 ff, 38, 83, 90 f
Compatibilism, 144–61
Compulsive neuroses, 105
Computers, 2
Concepts, 51, 135
Concomitants, 58
Concupiscentia (sense-desire), 50
Conditional analysis of ability, 140–142
Conditional commands, 75
Conduct, 16 f
Conflict of wants, 105, 116
Conscious acts, 53
Consciousness, 5, 47
Consent, 59, 62, 67
Consequences, 54 ff
Contraindications, 94
Contingency of practical reasoning, 23, 94 f
Control, 53
Corrupt councillor (example), 103
Covering law, 109, 146, 151
Criminal Justice Act, 1967, 62
Cross of Chelsea, L. J., 67

Darts (example), 136 f, 156
Davidson, D., 55, 108, 121, 141

Decision, 25, 40
Defeasibility, 23, 43, 92, 96, 115–17, 120
Deliberation, 14, 16, 22, 25
Descartes, 10, 12, 24, 50, 122
Desire, 49 ff; see sense-desire
Description (of action, of object, of volition), 51 ff, 95–8, 160; see level
Descriptions, Theory of, 77
Descriptive content, 40, 86
Determinism, 107, 111 ff, 145–61
Dice, 159 f
Dick and the slimmer (example), 199
Disposition v. episode, 15, 24, 123
Distribution of ability over disjunction, 138
Dog (example) 5, 15, 20, 42, 52, 143
Doxastic logic, 130, 139
Drowning child (example), 15
Duns Scotus, 156
Dynamic Modalities, 130 ff

Edwards, J., 141
Efficient cause, 108
Emotions, 40 f
Ends and means, 16, 17, 50 f
Entertaining a proposition, 36
Enthymeme, 91
Episode v. disposition, 15
Epistemic (logic, possibility, modality), 130 ff, 138
Exercise of a capacity, 10 f
Explanation, inference to, 89, 93
Expression 30–2, 35, 44; v. manifestation, 31, 51
External v. internal, 133
Extrovert v. introvert, 14, 23, 34

Faculty, 1, 4, 14
Falling tile (example), 55
Feinberg, J., 55
Felony, 66
Fiats, 39, 43, 74 ff, 90
Foresight v. intention, 57, 59, 67
Formation rules for logic of practical reasoning, 74–9

Formulation, 22
Frankfurt, H., 23
Frege, G., 8, 35 ff, 74, 86
Freud, S., 99 ff

Geach, P. T., 29, 92, 110, 111, 135
Generosity, 120
Gift of the gab (example), 11
Goals, 19, 47 ff, 80 f, 91
Goodness, 93 ff
Goddard, L. J., 61
Greek (French, German), ability to speak (example), 53, 123, 130, 135
Grievous bodily harm, 61 ff

Hailsham, L. J., 63 ff
Happiness, 21
Hare, R. M., 31, 39, 74, 77, 88–91, 103–5
Heart, saying in, 35
Herod (example), 84
Hexis, 123
Hintikka, J. K. K., 128
Historical inevitability, 155
Hobbes, T., 144, 146
Honoré, A. M., 131, 135
Horse to water (example), 129
Hotel booking (example), 90
Hume, D., 1, 10, 12, 108–11, 114–120, 122, 144
Humours, balancing of (example), 72
Hunger, 35, 49, 52, 120
Hypostatization, 10

'If I choose', 140
Imagination, 6 ff, 25, 35
Immortality, 9, 11
Imperatives, 34, 74, 85, 88
Imperative theory of the will, 28–45
Inability, psychological, 104
Inaugural lecture (example), 99
Incontinence, *see* akrasia
Inconsistency in practical reasoning, 90, 93
Indifference, 122 ff, 142–4, 146

Inductive logic, 88
Inevitability, 155
Inference, 70–96; *v.* truth, 85
Information, 34
Intelligence, 4
Intention, 18, 21, 25, 30 ff, 40, 53, 56–61, 98–101
Intentional 'under a description.' 98–100
Interference, 101, 109, 111–14, 115–16
Internal *v.* external, 31, 50, 133
Internal impressions, 12, 30
Introvert *v.* extrovert, 12–14, 15, 23
IRA (example), 67
Itch (example), 113 f

James II (example) 103
James, W., 12
Jigsaw (example), 150
Johnson, S., 1, 145 f
Judgement, 29, 40

Kilbrandon, L. J., 66
Kripke, S., 138

Labour candidate (example), 73
Law Commission, 67 f
Law, intention in, 59 ff
Letter posting (example), 73, 82
Leibniz, G. W., 102, 153
Levels of explanation and description, 149, 157
Lion (example), 52
Locke, D., 117–19
Locke, J., 143
Locked in room (example), 143
Logic of practical reasoning, 85 ff
Logic of satisfaction, 81 ff, 89, 91
Logic of satisfactoriness, 81ff, 89, 91
Logical constants, 74–6, 78
Logical truth, 85–7
London train (example), 70 f, 91 f, 102, 117
Looseness of link between reason and action, 101 ff
Lorry (example), 140

Lords, House of, 62 ff
Love letters (example), 65

Macaulay, Lord, 8, 103
Making up one's mind, 40
Malice aforethought, 59 ff
March (example), 88, 97
Martini (example), 133
Means and ends, 16, 17, 21, 55, 58, 95
Mechanism, mental, 118
Megarians, 126
Mens Rea, 59 ff, 67 ff
Mental acts, 6, 119
Mental arithmetic, 6 f
Mental events & states, 6, 118, 120
Midas, 84
Milk, sale of (example), 60
Mill, J. S., 109, 111 f, 116
Milton, J., 158
Mind, 2 ff
Mindszenty, Cardinal (example), 44
Mirror-image reasoning, 82
Modal logic, 130–40
Modus ponens, 70
Molina, L., 123
Monologue, inner, 6, 8, 35
Mood, 34, 40, 86
Muhammad Ali (example), 142
Multiplication table, 9
Murder, 59–69
Musical score (example), 36

Natural agency, kinds, and powers, 46, 127
Necessary conditions *v.* sufficient conditions, 88
Necessity in theoretical and practical reasoning, 71
Need, 48 f
Negligence, 60
Nero (example), 119
Neustic, 39
Niagara Falls (example), 136
Nobleness, 17
Nowell-Smith, P., 131, 141

Oblique causation, 121

Oblique intention, 59 ff
Occult powers, 15
Omnipotence, 134
Onus of match, 38
Opportunity, 123, 131–9, 141, 151
Optation, 43 f
Optative mood, 39
Orders *v.* commands, 31
Orexis, 16 f
Otherwise, ability to do, 141
'Ought', 103 f
Overdetermined actions 143

Packing suitcase (example), 90
Pain, 7
Pantomime, 32
Parallelogram of forces, 116
Paul and Abel (example), 71
Pears, D., 33 ff, 108, 111, 112
Penelhum, T., 25
Perception, 41 f
Performances *v.* states *v.* activities, 35, 54
Phrastics, 39 f, 74 ff, 86 f
Physiological determinism, 148 ff
Pius XII (example), 176
Plans and projects, 74, 80
Plans of life, 16–18
Plants, 143
Plato, 8, 9,
Play, 49
Poison (example), 108, 116
Policeman, killing of (example), 61
Pope (example), 28
Possible world semantics, 138
Powers, 46 f, 123 f; active *v.* passive, 123; innate *v.* acquired, 123; natural *v.* personal, 126 f, 129, 139, 141; rational *v.* nonrational, 53, 12
Practical inference, reasoning, 18, 22, 56, 70–96
Prayer, 34
Predication, 30
Predictability, 143
Prescriptivism, 103 f
Prohairesis, 16–18, 21, 98
Proposition, 43, 87

Propositions with two verbs, 41
Pros and cons, 95, 110
Psychoanalysis, 99–101
Psychological determinism, 111–13, 120, 148
Psychological inability, 104–6
Ptolemaic hypothesis, 93
Punishment, 105
Purpose, 58, 80 f
Putting (example), 141, 151

Quartermaster (example), 25
Queen Anne (example), 77

Randomness, 149, 159
Rational appetite, 23
Rational consideration, 21 f
Rational powers, 53, 124
Reasons, 20–2, 55 f; reasons *v.* causes, 107–11, 113–21
Reasonable man, 61
Reductionism, 10, 124, 128
Regress argument against volitions, 13, 17, 26, 31, 35, 147 f
Report *v.* expression, 40
Result *v.* consequence, 54 ff
River (example), 146 f
Risk, 64–8
Rock of Gilbraltar (example), 9
Round peg in round hole (example), 10
Ross, A., 84
Ross, D., 47
Russell, Lord, 41, 77
Ryle, G., 13–14, 24

Salvation, decree of (example), 158
Satisfaction, logic of, 81 ff
Satisfactoriness, logic of, 80–5, 88–93, 95
'Seize' (example), 136
Self-addressed commands, 32 f
Self-consciousness, 5
Self-evidence and self-desirability, 94
Self-exhortation, 33
Self-procured inclinations, 27
Sense-desire, 16, 49 f, 52, 104 ff

Senses, 49
Sentence-radical, *see* phrastic
Seriousness, 35 ff
Side-effects, 57 f
Sincerity, 30, 33
Smith, 61, 66
Smoking (example), 137, 139
Snoring (example), 53
Social science fiction, 110
Socrates, 47, 103
Specification of wants, 117
Speech-acts *v.* moods, 33, 34, 38
Spontaneity, 122 ff, 142–4, 140
Stalnaker, R., 140
Steane, 60
Steering wheel (example), 22
Stenius, E., 74, 86, 87
Step missing (example), 119
Stoutland, F., 92
Strength of wants, of will, 106 ff
Surgeon (example), 68
Symbols, 2, 3, 51
Syllogism, practical, 72 ff

Taylor, C., 56
Tendencies, 110 f
Tense logic, 130, 134
Terrorists, 68
Testimony, 42
Thought, 12, 23
Tolstoy, L., 145, 160
Toolmaking, 5
Train (example), 20
Transcendentalism, 11, 124, 128
Tropic, 39 f, 74 ff, 78
Troy, fall of (example), 16, 42
Truth, 43, 79, 86; in logic, 85 ff; descriptive *v.* modal, 86
Truth-tables, 79, 82, 85

Umbrella (example), 38
Unconscious intention, 99–101
Uninsured use of motor (example), 60
Utterance, mental, 29

Vehicle *v.* exercise, 10 f
Vickers, 61, 63, 66

Virtus dormitiva, 126
Volition, 16, 26, 29, 30, 34, 40
Volition, Humean, 12 f, 23 f 25, 30, 41
Voluntariness, 4, 13, 15, 16, 18, 19, 21; *v.* intentionality 18 f, 53 f
Von Wright, G. H., 54, 71, 82, 84, 130

Wanting, 25, 29, 58, 118; volition *v.* desire, 16, 51

Weakness of will, *see* akrasia
Will, 20, 42 & *passim*
Willingness, 41, 59
Window opening (example), 54, 57, 74, 83, 91
Wiggins, 154
Wittgenstein, 29, 36, 85, 125, 127

Yawning (example), 53, 58